Good Morning, Life!

One Woman Waking Up to Happiness,
One Moment at a Time

BARBARA DEMONE

 FriesenPress

Suite 300 - 990 Fort St
Victoria, BC, V8V 3K2
Canada

www.friesenpress.com

Copyright © 2020 by Barbara Demone
First Edition — 2020

All rights reserved.

No part of this publication may be reproduced in any form, or by any means, electronic or mechanical, including photocopying, recording, or any information browsing, storage, or retrieval system, without permission in writing from FriesenPress.

ISBN
978-1-5255-8235-6 (Hardcover)
978-1-5255-8236-3 (Paperback)
978-1-5255-8237-0 (eBook)

1. *Body, Mind & Spirit, Mindfulness & Meditation*

Distributed to the trade by The Ingram Book Company

To Carter and Austin, you are bright lights in my life, my loves, and the best teachers I could ask for.

Contents

Preface	1
Welcome, friend!	1
Introduction	5
The Million-Dollar Question	5
A Happiness Mindset	15
Who: The Real Me	17
What: Mindful Awareness	25
Why: A Wake-up Call	35
When: The Present Moment	43
How: Mindful Journaling	47
Waking Up: The Journal	51
Awake: My Happiness Formula	151
Epilogue: Solid, Solid, Solid	161
Acknowledgments	163
Notes	167

Preface

Welcome, friend!

Just like you, I am an ordinary person with a busy life, juggling various roles—to name a couple of my own, mother and full-time career woman. My weekdays are a steady stream of activities: getting my two kids' butts out of bed and off to school, commuting, then a non-stop day at work. In the past, these hectic days would fly by, leaving me exhausted and less than satisfied. By the evening, my patience was short and I was quick to yell, trying to hurry my kids to bed so I could squeeze in some final household chores. My life was packed with great things, but I seemed to be living so much of it on autopilot, not truly experiencing each moment, not really enjoying it.

And then it happened. I uncovered a powerful secret that changed my life.

I discovered how to live each day in peace and happiness. Yes, even in the midst of a working mom's chaos! I didn't have to change my life—just my mindset. It's a journey and it takes continued practice, but it's absolutely worth it. I'd love to share my secret with you.

Around ten years ago, I began learning about mindful awareness in my quest to find happiness. As I practised mindfulness throughout the day, I realized that there was a huge gap between theory and practical life experience. It was difficult to stay mindful when my kids fought or when a colleague undermined my team's efforts in a meeting. It was when I started writing a daily mindfulness journal during my morning commute that my project really gained traction. As I practised mindfulness in this way, I discovered that it really works. Although I did not originally set out to write a book, the journal evolved into what you're holding in your hands. This life-changing shift in mindset is easily attainable. If I can do it, I know anyone can.

I am not a dedicated mindfulness teacher who spends many hours in meditation or on retreats. I'm simply applying the principles set out by trusted visionaries, whom you may be familiar with. My main teachings come from authors Eckhart Tolle *(The Power of Now: A Guide to Spiritual Enlightenment and A New Earth: Awakening to Your Life's Purpose)* and Dr. Shefali Tsabary *(The Conscious Parent: Transforming Ourselves, Empowering Our Children)*. I have also found inspiration and guidance from other spiritual teachers, such as Buddhist monk and peace activist Thich Nhat Hanh, as well as leadership and business experts, including Stephen R. Covey *(The 7 Habits of Highly Effective People: Powerful Lessons in Personal Change)*, and psychologists like Shawn Achor *(The Happiness Advantage: How a Positive Brain Fuels Success in Work and Life)*.

I continue to practise daily, gleaning new lessons as I go. As you'll see, some days I'm able to be a little more mindful than others, but I learn from failing too (in fact, bad days are better teachers than good ones). Each moment, whether I do well or not-so-well, is valuable in bridging the gap between performing routines on autopilot and waking up to the essence of life—one that is full, meaningful, and happy.

I'm excited for you to join me on the journey!

With love and gratitude,

Barbara

Introduction

The Million-Dollar Question

If you want to be happy, be.

—Leo Tolstoy

Recently, I attended my twenty-year business school reunion. I went to university with some pretty impressive individuals whom I knew would become very successful. And they are. Around forty of us spent an evening together consisting of a lovely dinner at a nice restaurant, followed by trying to relive our school years barhopping and doing a few too many tequila shots. Throughout the evening, rumours circulated about how successful certain old classmates were. Apparently, one of them practically owned the city, as his real estate investment company managed most of the properties downtown. His connections came in handy when we found ourselves in a long lineup in front of a bar: he pulled some strings and we were granted immediate entry. Another bit of gossip regarded the net worth of a successful entrepreneur and hedge fund manager—several million dollars to be sure. It was a fun evening, and certainly interesting to observe the types of topics our conversations circled around. We boasted about each others' careers and families, and generally how well we were doing in life, especially from the outside.

The most meaningful conversation was had the following day, when a small group of us strolled around campus. We were five healthy adults, all (seemingly) happily married with children, beautiful homes, and successful careers. Along with me, a bank regulator, there was a marketing exec, an HR professional, a venture capital investor, and the hedge fund manager we'd gossiped about the night before. It was a beautiful, sunny Sunday morning. A bit hungover, we meandered around the old campus buildings, sharing memories. As we chatted, a simple question was posed to the group by the hedge fund manager.

"Are you happy?"

There was a pause. I was quiet. Inside I knew my own answer, which was a big "Yes", as this was a topic I had focused on over the last ten years. I was keenly interested in what the others had to say. A variety of vague responses emerged:

"Well, my job is pretty engaging. I just wish I had more time with my kids."

"I never seem to have enough time in my days. But I have everything I need to be happy."

"Well, everything was going very well in my life, but then I took on this new role, and while it's interesting, I lost some of the balance I had. I used to cook dinner every night, which I really enjoyed. Now I don't have time, and I miss it."

Life is what I am experiencing at this very instant. Outside of the thoughts in my mind, which all too often focus on the past and the future, there really is nothing else. The present moment is all I have.

Sitting in that chair, I felt a new aliveness. I'd just discovered a massive secret. How many other people knew that secret? How many people didn't know it, like me just moments before? It was as if the world had shifted beneath me. The room I was in was still the same. My baby was the same, and I was physically the same. The change was inside of me. It was my perspective that had altered, my mindset. And that, I discovered, makes all the difference.

A Quest for Happiness

With that realization, my quest for true happiness began. The questions started flowing. If this is life . . .

Am I where I truly want to be?
Who am I, really?
What is my life's purpose?
And the biggie: am I truly happy?

To these questions, all I had was a big fat "I don't know." That didn't satisfy me. If this is the one life I have, I needed a better answer. I couldn't think of anything more important.

That day, I realized that I had been preparing for life for years. I am naturally ambitious, so I tend to fixate on the next steps to take to get ahead. I largely saw high school as a means to an end, more focused on getting good marks than on enjoying learning about new topics. I did have favourite subjects—math and business—but for the others, I just crammed for exams to get the marks I needed.

The hedge fund manager offered his own reply, "My job is pretty stressful right now. I never know if I'm making the right decisions. My family seems happy. I don't know, though, my kids are growing so fast. My teenager is hard to read."

We all agreed that we enjoyed travelling and felt lucky that we'd had some fun travel opportunities. But the question of happiness still hung in the air, not fully answered.

Why, despite having many things that one might equate to a happy life—great jobs, healthy families, beautiful homes, physical and political safety—did my colleagues not have an easy, heartfelt, resounding "YES!" to the question of happiness?

The conversation took me back to a day more than ten years prior. The year was 2008. I was sitting in a rocking chair in my son Carter's bedroom. Carter was just a few months old and quite a demanding baby. He wanted to breastfeed constantly, so I was trapped in that rocking chair for the good part of a year. Oprah had chosen Eckhart Tolle's *A New Earth* for her latest book club selection and was hosting a web series with the author. I read the book and tuned into the webinars, which included topics like how to quiet the mind, how to put the ego in check and how to be fully present in the moment. One day, as I was contemplating these concepts, it just hit me.

This is it. Life. It is happening. Now.

It was what Oprah calls an "Aha" moment, an epiphany. It suddenly seemed so simple and obvious. Why hadn't I seen it this way before? Why hadn't anyone smacked me and made me realize this simple truth? **Life is not about the future, it is about now.**

My future plans took precedence over curiosity, over learning, over living in the moment. My goals: acing exams, then on to the next grade, then to university, leading to a full-time job. And once I had the job, my focus was set on getting promoted to the next level. I never felt settled or at ease, as I was always searching, striving, anticipating.

This doesn't mean I would have described myself as unhappy, though. From childhood to adulthood, my life was filled with moments I called "happy."

As a kid, when I was asked to recall my happiest moments, I invariably cited a visit to Canada's Wonderland. The sense of freedom and excitement on roller coasters, speeding through the air with the wind in my face, is what I equated to happiness at the time. The speed was exhilarating; it was just over too soon. It was a fleeting happiness, not a lasting feeling.

In my teens and twenties, I knew how to have fun. I had an active weekend party schedule through high school, university, and beyond. Many pleasant evenings were spent hanging out with friends, drinking. Mind you, they were often followed by nasty hangovers and less-than-productive days. If I'm honest with myself, those nights were about searching—for a boyfriend at bars and clubs, for acceptance from friends and acquaintances, for excitement. Partying was definitely fun, but it wasn't exactly a stable state of peace and contentment.

The word for "happy" in most languages comes from the word "lucky." What role has luck played in my happiness, if any? The answer is trickier than it seems. In my graduating year at university, we were wined and dined by big accounting firms to entice us to join them. I chose Arthur Andersen because of its reputation for high standards and professionalism, and because of the people I met. A few short years after I had started working there, the firm went out of business, convicted of obstruction of justice for shredding documents related to its audit of Enron. Finding myself out of a job early in my career, I considered myself unlucky. My friends rallied around me in support. Indeed, it was through friends that I found my next position—a role that would lead to my present career. Without that bit of "unluckiness," I wouldn't have found such a great fit within my current organization. I now think of the term "luck" as a misnomer, a judgment I am not fit to make, as I don't know how life will unfold. Events and circumstances that may first appear to be unlucky may in fact turn out to be positive developments.

Years later, I had a good job, a loving husband, financial security, a nice house, a decent car—everything I needed. But my happiness was tinged with insecurity. It depended on the good things I had in my life. What if those things went away? What if I lost my job, or my marriage fell apart? How could I possibly be happy then? My happiness was precarious, a little scary even. It did not feel solid and grounded.

Are We Happy?

The importance of happiness in human life was recognized by the United Nations General Assembly when they declared March 20 as World Happiness Day, highlighting "the relevance of happiness and well-being as universal goals and aspirations in the lives of human beings around the world."[1]

Indeed, what better life could we ask for than to spend each day feeling happy?

And yet, there is a lot of evidence to suggest that we are in the midst of an unhappiness epidemic. Here are a few studies that demonstrate our collective struggle:

- A 2010 survey by The Conference Board, a not-for-profit research organization, found that only 45 percent of workers were happy at their jobs, the lowest in over two decades.[2]
- Depression rates have risen tenfold since 1960.[3]
- Fifty years ago, the average age of onset of depression was 29. Today, it is 14 years old.[4]
- A person living in a Western culture is about four to ten times more likely to develop clinical depression or anxiety than a person in an Eastern culture.[5]
- According to a 2020 survey, 22 percent of millennials say they have no friends.[6]
- A Deloitte study estimates that due to the coronavirus pandemic, 6.3 million to 10.7 million Canadians will visit a doctor for mental health issues, a 54 to 163 percent increase from pre-pandemic levels.[7]

Given that happiness is a society-wide crisis, is focusing on my own personal happiness a worthwhile pursuit? Absolutely. First, my own happiness is all that lies within my control. I can't force anyone else to be happy. Second, collective happiness is made up of the happiness of individuals within the whole. By improving my own happiness, I impact the collective because positivity has a ripple effect.

When our society is plunging into a downward spiral of unhappiness, it's time to look closely at what happiness really means.

What is True Happiness?

Throughout my life, I have certainly experienced many feelings of happiness, but with missing pieces to the whole I call **true happiness**, a state that is:

- Characterized by peace and contentment;
- Long-lasting, not a fleeting pleasure;
- Not conditional on the things I have acquired or the roles that I play;
- Not conditional upon a future state or goal;
- Not dependent on, or characterized by, luck.

To put it more simply, true happiness is **a state of inner peace.**

There is some overlap here with other definitions of happiness. The Merriam-Webster Dictionary defines it as "a **state of well-being and contentment: joy.**"[8]

Dr. Shefali Tsabary, psychologist and author, talks about happiness as "an **internal state of bliss** that is always available to us."[9]

Eckhart Tolle, spiritual teacher and bestselling author of *The Power of Now*, describes life flowing with **joy and ease** when unhappiness and struggle dissolves.[10]

Positive psychologists generally agree on what happiness feels like—satisfied with life, good mood, positive emotions, enjoyment, etc. A distinction is made between happiness and pleasure: pleasure is defined as a momentary sensory experience, whereas happiness is **a more stable state**.[11]

Fortunately for us, happiness can be purposefully and systematically developed through a change in mindset. In *Buddha's Brain:*

The Practical Neuroscience of Happiness, Love and Wisdom, Rick Hanson, PhD and Richard Mendius, MD write, "Only we humans worry about the future, regret the past, and blame ourselves for the present. We get frustrated when we can't have what we want, and disappointed when what we like ends. We suffer *that* we suffer. We get upset about being in pain, angry about dying, sad about waking up sad yet another day. This kind of suffering—which encompasses most of our unhappiness and dissatisfaction—is constructed by the brain. It is made up. Which is ironic, poignant—and supremely hopeful. **For if the brain is the cause of suffering, it can also be the cure.**"[12]

Psychologist Shawn Achor also discusses happiness as something that can be increased via actionable steps. In his book *The Happiness Advantage*, he writes, "Waiting to be happy limits our brain's potential for success, whereas cultivating positive brains makes us more motivated, efficient, resilient, creative, and productive."[13]

In this book I share my personal journey to inner peace, fulfillment, and enjoyment of daily life in the real world. The path to a strong, resounding "Yes!" to that simple question, "Are you happy?" An unconditional Yes, with no strings attached. A deep-seated Yes that doesn't depend on anyone or anything.

This is my answer to the million-dollar question: **what's the formula for true happiness?**

So let's get to it. Here's the Who, What, Why, When and How of changing mindset through mindful awareness to bring about true happiness.

A Happiness Mindset

There is no way to happiness; happiness is the way.

—Thich Nhat Hanh

Who: The Real Me

The one thing I know for sure is that you cannot even begin to live your best life without being connected to your spirit.

—Oprah

Among my many roles are wife, mother, sister, daughter, niece, aunt, friend, and bank regulator. Connection is important to me, and I have strong relationships with many of the people in my life. I have a wonderful husband (my high school sweetheart) and two energetic, creative, and caring boys whom I adore immensely. My extended family is fairly large, and childhood friends continue to be an important part of my life.

I grew up in a rural home just outside a small town northwest of Toronto. School was always something I enjoyed, and I graduated from university with a focus on business and accounting. I now live in the suburbs in a large town just outside Toronto, and commute daily to the city by train. I have a leadership role in the financial services industry. The government organization I work for regulates banks, insurance companies, and pension plans. And yes, I do love my job! Some of my passions are working out, hiking, meditating, reading, travelling, and hanging out with my friends and family.

Who am I? There's a quick bio. But I realize that it's a pretty superficial answer. I understand that you can't really know me just by reading a few facts about my background and some of my experiences. You could, however, make some assumptions or judgments about me. And speaking of judgments, I can make judgments about myself too—thanks to the ego.

Ego

Ego is self-image, a **picture in my mind** of myself. It's how I perceive "Barbara Demone," the individual, separate from other people. From my ego, my sense of self-worth and self-esteem arise. Many elements go into the creation of this picture, but essentially, it comes from my own mind.

As Eckhart Tolle writes, "The most common ego identifications have to do with possessions, the work you do, social status and recognition, knowledge and education, physical appearance, special abilities, relationships, personal and family history, belief systems and often also political, nationalistic, racial, religious and other collective identifications. None of these is you."[14] Following Tolle's description, my mental selfie is coloured by the roles I play (mom, bank regulator), my personality (perfectionist, empathetic), past experiences (graduated university, traveled to various countries), and so on.

In the little bio I shared earlier, I included mainly positive information about me. There's my ego at play, striving to maintain a positive self-image. So what happens when circumstances conflict with that positive picture? Early in my career, I failed a major exam for the Chartered Accountant designation and also lost my job. Needless to say, this was a difficult time. I had always considered myself a great student, and successful in my work. So it felt awful when I failed that exam. It distorted that perfect egoic image I had kept well-polished. I identified as an accountant, and now I was at risk of losing that identity. Interesting that I didn't include that tidbit in my bio.

That was a pretty big event, but there are many less dramatic, day-to-day situations when my ego can be triggered. Say my son has a temper tantrum in the grocery store, but I see myself as an effective mother who is always in control of her child's behaviour. The tantrum shatters that self-image—I'm not who I thought after all. When reality conflicts with a self-image it can create discomfort and unhappiness.

My sense of self is also <u>influenced by others'</u> views of me. This must be why I often hear advice about <u>the importance of surrounding ourselves with positive people</u>. My ego judges me, but we judge each other as well. I recently experienced this at work, when a colleague spread rumours about me and my team, criticizing our work. Based on her judgment, I found my thoughts skewing in a negative direction too. My mindfulness practice came in handy here, as I noticed myself having these sorts of thoughts. It doesn't mean it was easy to change their direction, though. It's amazing how powerful thought habits can be—more on that later.

Understanding the ego was an important step for me in my happiness journey. My fundamental lesson: **whatever mental image I have of myself is not actually who I am**. I am so much more than a mind's perception—either mine or others'. How freeing! Knowing this allows me to more easily accept unexpected events without making harsh judgments of myself, others, or the situation itself. I take myself less seriously and do things that I held back from in the past because I was worried about what people might think of me. One of my fitness goals is to take 10,000 steps a day. While I wait for my morning train on the platform, I walk back and forth or go up and down the stairs to get some of those steps in. While it may look strange to the other commuters and they may judge me for it, I sometimes get up to 2,000 steps (according to my Fitbit)! Accomplishing a decent chunk of my goal early in the day feels like a big win. I can let go of the fear associated with protecting a certain image of myself, knowing the image is not real, but imagined. I can intentionally focus on my goals without letting perceptions limit me.

With this mind shift, I have also become better at delivering presentations at work. I can more easily focus on connecting with the people I'm presenting to and ensure that my content is clear. Previously, I've been more focused on myself, worried about how it'll look if I mess up. When my ego was in the way, presentations were much more stressful, much less fun, and no doubt less effective.

Social media, depending on its use, can be an external depiction of our egos at play. As we can carefully craft our profile and the image that is portrayed to the world based on what we post. As we know, this is not who we are. We are much deeper.

Practicing mindful awareness allows me to identify when my ego is triggered. I can then stop and let go of the identification with thoughts before I react. Connecting with others in a deeper way is also possible when I am aware of the ego. I know that behaviour and reactions do not define who a person is and I don't take things personally. With the knowledge that the ego is not real, I can go beyond it and act from my deeper self, resulting in inner peace and happiness.

Life Situation

Along with ego, I discovered another key player in the question of happiness: external factors and situations. I was introduced to the concept of *life situation* by, once again, Eckhart Tolle. He describes the difference between *life* and *life situation* as this:

> Your life situation exists in time. Your life is now.
> Your life situation is mind-stuff. Your life is real.[15]

So, *life* is who you are. Fundamentally, who you are is indescribable—you are simply *life*. The fact that you are breathing, for example, is part of your life.

Life situation, on the other hand, comprises external factors we can use to describe ourselves and the kind of life we lead. Psychologist Roger Allen, PhD, elaborates:

> My life situation has to do with what is going on "out there"—events, day-to-day occurrences, global circumstances that affect us all (economy, state of the world) and personal circumstances that affect just me and perhaps my loved ones. My life, on the other hand, is much more than my life situation. It begins with the very fact of life. Here I am—an incredibly complex living and breathing being which not only miraculously sustains life but interprets, makes sense, and chooses how to respond to life (or my life situation). This "being" (life) is so much more and bigger than my life situation.[16]

The information I shared in my bio, then—married, live in the suburbs, etc.—describes my life situation. This distinction, I realized, is a very important factor in determining my happiness. If I depend on life situation for happiness, then happiness is conditional.

Conditional happiness has created significant anxiety for me in the past. When Todd and I decided we were ready to be parents and started trying to conceive, many months passed without any luck. With each negative pregnancy test, my anxiety rose. What if I couldn't conceive? My dream of being a parent wouldn't be realized. What would people think of me when all my friends had beautiful families full of children running around the yard? How would I fit in? Parenthood was not part of my life situation, but I wanted it desperately; my happiness depended upon it. My ego flared up and harsh, judgmental words blazed in my mind—*barren, barren*—making me feel less than worthy. Swept up in negative thoughts, I compared myself to friends who'd conceived without even trying. But what was keeping me from happiness—my life situation or my thoughts about it? In previous years, I didn't have any children, and yet I felt quite content. It was my ego's interpretation of the situation that caused my unhappiness.

I now recognize that defining myself by external factors is a trap, because guess what? Circumstances can and will change. If I am too attached to any of these, I am more likely to perceive change as a crisis. Life situation cannot reliably define who I am. For a more resilient happiness, I need a stronger anchor. My happiness is not dependent on whether I have children, have a certain job, or am in a particular relationship. It is more reliant on the choice I make to be happy and on my ability to not let my mind inhibit that inner peace with stories and negative thoughts.

Maybe there are limited words to describe who I really am, and that's okay. I am much more nuanced than labels; I am a **being**. As I wake up, I get in touch with my true self, my deepest essence, me beyond definition. This is what makes me the same person today that I was when I was a baby. When I recognize this place and live from it, these are the moments when I transcend my ego.

What: Mindful Awareness

*The present moment is filled with joy and happiness.
If you are attentive, you will see it.*

—Thich Nhat Hanh

When I first learned about the ego, I started to understand just how powerful my mind's influence over how I experience daily life is. How busy my mind is! Thoughts are continuously interrupting my consciousness. An example of my thought patterns during a typical workday:

The alarm clock goes off. I hit the snooze button, not once, not twice, but three times. Finally noticing the time, I jump out of bed. *Oh no, I'm going to be late and miss my train. Why didn't I just get up when the alarm went off? Am I lazy?* While I'm brushing my teeth: *What am I going to wear? I'd love to wear my blue skirt, but it fits a bit tight now. I should have woken up early this morning to exercise since I didn't last night. Okay, so the blue skirt is out, what about my grey pants? I just wore them two days ago. I think I need to go shopping. I don't have enough nice clothes. But there's never enough time for it. Maybe I should go shopping at lunch. No, that won't work.*

Back-to-back meetings all day. I never have enough time to do everything I need to do.

I finish brushing my teeth, barely noticing whether I have actually brushed them. On my drive over to the train station, my thoughts flow in a continuous stream. Perhaps I don't notice my friend walking her dog on the sidewalk, or the vibrant yellow flowers and ornamental grasses swaying in the wind.

Through the day I float from meeting to meeting. On the train ride home, my mind is shrouded in the work day behind me, replaying conversations. *Did Fred misinterpret what I said in that meeting? Did he think I was criticizing him? I hope not. I only meant to make a point and draw attention to an issue that was nobody's fault. Shoot, I should have started off by acknowledging the hard work Fred did. Should I send an email to apologize? Maybe I should ask Sue if she interpreted it that way. Oh no, I think I forgot to respond to Joe's email. Did he say he needed a response by the end of today or the end of the week? I'll have to respond tonight just in case.* When I finally get off the train, I barely remember the trip at all.

Why do we so love to dwell on worries and stresses? Our brains have a negativity bias—they are drawn to bad news. We are much more likely to detect, emphasize, and retain negative information than positive information.[17] No wonder we face an uphill battle to get to a happy state. While the workday in my example likely involved some really positive events—a wonderful chat with a colleague over coffee, a successful presentation, a number of fruitful coaching discussions—if left to its own devices, my mind tends to gloss over them. I could pat myself on the back for the good work I did and appreciate the new things that I learned, but it's easier to stress over details and find faults in my achievements.

Interestingly, thoughts and psychological pain trigger the same neural networks that *physical* pain does. This is because the amygdala, which is a central processor in the brain for emotional responses, sets off the same alarms whether the threat is real or perceived (i.e., only in my head).[18] Intentionally moving our attention away from negative thought patterns can help us both mentally and physically.

What is Mindful Awareness?

The aim of mindful awareness, or mindfulness, is to be aware of the present moment and practise living in the "here and now." It involves noticing the sights and sounds around me, my feelings, and my own body. Oftentimes, my thoughts take me out of the present moment by focusing on the past and future. I get lost in them. And this tendency is not unique to my experience. When I listen to a yoga instructor encouraging her students to break away from the thought train and come back to the breath, I know that it's not just me.

The good news is that practising mindfulness helps us become aware of our thoughts, giving us a fighting chance to prevent them from running the show. We can replace negative thoughts with positive or neutral ones and free ourselves from anxious thought patterns. We can quite literally change the brain thanks to its neuroplasticity. In a famous study, researchers studied the brains of taxi drivers in London, whose job requires them to remember the city's maze-like layout of winding streets, not at all the grid system of cities like New York. Looking at the hippocampus, the part of the brain responsible for visual and spatial memory, the researchers found that these taxi drivers had a much larger hippocampus than the average.[19] Why? The drivers exercised this part of the brain so frequently. They had built it up through practice. Another study came to similar conclusions about the brain's ability to change, finding that "as you become a happier person, the left frontal region of your brain becomes more active."[20]

When I was introduced to mindfulness, the first exercise I did was to sit very still in a chair, close my eyes, and bring attention to my hands. I didn't move or touch them—I simply felt the sensation of my hands for a good two minutes. Since it's impossible to think of more than one thing at a time, while my attention was on my hands, my mind was quiet. I wasn't thinking, planning, daydreaming, or worrying. It felt like a lovely break for my mind and body. After those two minutes, I slowly moved my attention to my arms. What did they feel like? I continued to scan each body part, then concentrated on my whole body, all at once. I felt my body sitting in that chair, in that moment. I felt a tingling sensation. My heart rate slowed and my breathing deepened. My mind and body were in partnership.

When I opened my eyes, I was much more aware of my surroundings. I really looked at the pictures on the wall, the colour of the paint. The carpet, which had a slight discolouration around the spot a table used to sit. I breathed in deeply and used each sense in turn. I sniffed. Nothing notable, but an observation nonetheless. I listened intently. It was a quiet mid-afternoon day in the suburbs. Carter was napping in my lap. I heard his breathing. I felt his warm body gently rising and falling with each breath.

In and out.
In and out.
A hum from the air conditioner.
Here and there, the sounds of birds chirping.

A calm feeling washed over me.

That was when I realized the power of the present moment. Right now. With no expectations of the next moment, no worry about past moments. The moment I am in right now is so peaceful and so wonderful. There is nothing wrong with it at all.

The thoughts in my mind cause me so much needless suffering. Suffering arises from rumination on past and future moments. The more I can focus my attention on the present moment, the happier I will be.

As I type these words, I am aware of my fingers moving on the keyboard—the posture of my spine in the chair I am sitting in—my boys' voices as they play a computer game. I notice when my mind wanders into future worry mode. *What if this book isn't any good? What if no one reads it? What if it's too personal and people judge me?* Just because I practise mindfulness doesn't mean that these sorts of thoughts stop coming. But I am more often aware of them when they arise. When I feel a quickened heartbeat or a tightness in my stomach, I recognize the signs that I have gotten lost in anxious thoughts. Physical reactions are a signal to pause and come back to the present moment. To remind myself that everything is okay. To come into my body, feel the sensation of my hands. Sometimes I just look out the window and notice a leaf on a tree . . . a squirrel scurrying by . . . a bird soaring through the air. Nature is a simple yet powerful guide to the present moment. Back to peace.

Before starting a mindfulness practice, my thoughts seemed to be an inextricable part of me. They simply couldn't be helped. Now, I recognize my thoughts as being separate from who I truly am. We all have the same types of anxious thought patterns, so there is no need to feel scared, threatened, or unique in having them. I can control them, or at least not let them control me. I can befriend my mind by getting to know it and show it how best to support me. When I am lost in thought, it is like an important part of me is asleep. Coming into the present moment is a lot like waking up.

Mindful Awareness in the Presence of Others

Being mindfully aware around other people is tricky, as it creates plenty of opportunities for my ego to be triggered. If someone's behaviour challenges my self-image or sense of worth, it's easy to react from a place of ego.

I have a colleague who tends to cut me off in meetings. Feeling disrespected, my ego snaps into defense mode. I might raise my voice and speak faster to get myself heard. The more I practise mindfulness, however, the more aware I am of the kinds of people and situations that trigger my ego. When I recognize the pattern playing out, I have the option of relaxing into the present moment. Experience shows that if I stay present and curious with even the harshest of individuals, I can actually have a decent encounter with them. When I'm cut off, if I pause, let them finish their sentence, then calmly ask if I may finish what I was saying, it's much more effective than cutting back in and forcing my point across.

Being aware of my expectations of others also helps to cut down on the drama. It's easy to expect other people to behave as I would in a particular situation. But I try to keep in mind that each of us has our own personal background, upbringing, and experiences. It's natural that we will each act differently in a given scenario. Getting frustrated by others' choices doesn't help anyone, particularly myself. So I don't put so much focus on my expectations. Why get so annoyed when someone cuts me off in traffic? Their behaviour is theirs and mine is mine. I can only control my own actions—not anyone else's. My happiness doesn't depend on what someone else did or didn't do. If someone's behaviour is rude or out of line, I have the option of telling them that I think it's inappropriate or taking action in some way. But I can also choose to let it go and not to harbour hard feelings that I then gossip and vent about. Gossiping and venting create a negative cycle of drama and unhappiness.

Being mindful in conversation with others can be a wonderful way to deepen a relationship. As a chatty extrovert, I can easily dominate a conversation if I let myself. I've learned to hold back more and listen without judgment, without preparing what I'll say in return. I might have created stories in my mind about the person, such as a past hurt provoked by a conversation we had. If these stories arise, I try to bring awareness to them, then move on.

While I believe we are becoming a more mindful society, we still have a long way to go. Wherever people identify with their thoughts, operate from a place of ego, and react based on their fears, staying in the present moment among others is an extra challenge.

Expectations and Intentions

Part of my mindfulness practice has been to get in touch with my purpose. What are my core values? My strengths? What brings me joy?

I used to do things simply because I thought that I should. If my friends were into cooking up feasts, for instance, I felt some kind of unspoken expectation—whether real or imagined—to do the same. I don't particularly enjoy cooking and I'm not a great cook. But when Todd and I were a young couple, many of our friends would hold lavish dinner parties. When it came our turn to host, I'd get stressed out, feeling pressured to come up with a unique gourmet meal to serve our guests. I'd spend so much time worrying about the food prior to the party, and then fret my way through the event itself, wondering if it was good enough.

But what are parties for, at the heart? What is my main objective in gathering with my friends? Spending time with people who are dear to me and showing them that they are important to me. At those dinner parties, I was so busy focusing on culinary expectations that I lost sight of my purpose. Stress gets in the way of connection. I could have enjoyed those evenings so much more with a change in approach. Nowadays, I prioritize quality time with friends over unrealistic expectations. When it is my turn to entertain, I either plan a simple recipe—or more typically, order in. My time is limited, so I make decisions that align with my purpose and bring me joy. A friend of mine recently commented that she hasn't ever had my cooking. Yes, my friend, that's by design, and I'm happier for it.

Leaving Room for Mistakes

I don't think anyone around me is perfect or needs to be, but it's oh-so-tempting to expect perfection of myself. Cultivating inner peace requires a shift in mindset: from uncompromising personal standards to forgiveness of my mistakes. A mistake is not a blemish in my value as a person, but an opportunity to learn. Making an effort and doing my best is all I can ask of myself. Toltec spiritual teacher Don Miguel Ruiz offers "Always Do Your Best" as one of his four tenets of moral conduct in his book *The Four Agreements*. He writes, "Under any circumstance, always do your best, no more and no less. But keep in mind that your best is never going to be the same from one moment to the next. Everything is alive and changing all the time, so your best will sometimes be high quality and other times it will not be as good."²¹ This liberating perspective creates space to learn from my errors, to observe my shortcomings with a lighter heart, and to feel satisfied with my actions, even when the results aren't optimal.

No matter what's currently going on in my life, the same old cycle is at play: thoughts generate feelings, which in turn impact my actions. Bringing awareness to my thoughts gives me more agency in this cycle. I can break free from ego patterns, judgments, and expectations, and just **be**, in this moment. My thoughts are like clouds covering a clear blue sky. I simply need to let the clouds roll by to experience the peace and happiness waiting behind.

Why: A Wake-up Call

The purpose of our lives is to be happy.

—The Dalai Lama

The Benefits of Happiness

The rewards of embarking on a personal journey of mindful awareness are rich indeed:

- experiencing everyday life with **greater ease and simplicity**;
- increased **acceptance** of the variety of life situations that come our way; greater **resilience** in handling challenges;
- **acting in alignment with our values**, with less guilt and fewer regrets;
- a deeper sense of **gratitude** for the good things in life;
- unshakeable **self-esteem**—without taking ourselves too seriously;
- more **harmonious relationships** and closer bonds with others;
- **enhanced openness to learning** and personal growth;
- feeling engaged and **successful** in our professional projects;
- an overall sense of being **settled, satisfied, and content**.

If this isn't enough to convince you, happiness is rewarding in the work sphere as well. As Shawn Achor writes in *The Happiness Advantage*, happiness fuels success. Contrary to conventional wisdom, which posits that if we work really hard, we'll be successful, and happy as a result, it's quite the opposite. Recent research in the field of positive psychology shows that when we are happy, we are more engaged in our work, more motivated, and more creative, resulting in increased productivity and professional success.[22]

The cherry on the sundae: impressive physical benefits. According to James Fowler, a political scientist at the University of California San Diego, "Happiness has been shown to have an important effect on reduced mortality, pain reduction, and improved cardiac function."[23]

Obstacles to Uncovering Happiness

While the benefits of living a more fulfilling and happy life are easy to say yes to, we may doubt that the dream of happiness is achievable. If happiness is impossible, why bother working for it? We may think that we can't expect always to be happy because life events are out of our control and bad things will certainly happen. How will we be happy if someone close to us dies, for instance? Indeed, it would be awkward to boast of being happy at such a time. But let's return to my definition of happiness: *a state of inner peace*. This state leaves room for serenity and sadness to coexist. If we are able to accept that death is an inevitable part of life, we can experience feelings of sadness alongside an enduring sense of inner peace.

Even if we do believe that happiness is attainable, the reality is that change can be hard. Status quo is easy, comfortable . . . known.

We have momentum in doing what we've always done, living how we've always lived. What if, in our attempt to reorient ourselves, we lose precious parts of our lives? A job? Friends? These worries are normal.

I am going to be honest. For most of my life, I had a superstition that if I was too happy, something bad would happen. Happiness was akin to tempting fate. To be safe, I would gently hold myself back from feeling too happy. I have no idea where that thought came from, but I now know that "good" things will happen, "bad" things will happen, and I am well equipped to handle them in mindful awareness. "Good" and "bad" are just labels we use. The more I am able to fully experience each moment as it is, the more alive I feel.

Finding a Wake-up Call

The mind is strong and stubborn. If it resists the idea of happiness or fears change, we may never leave square one. For many of us, a wake-up call provides a necessary push onto the path toward happiness.

For my active, baseball-loving Uncle Bert, it was Amyotrophic Lateral Sclerosis (ALS). He was just thirty-nine when he was diagnosed with this disease, which gradually paralyzes the body as the brain loses the ability to communicate with the muscles. Typically, people with ALS die within two to five years of being diagnosed.

My uncle had a tough childhood and became essentially homeless when he was just sixteen years old. At the age of twenty-five, his beloved wife, who suffered a postpartum psychosis, died from an overdose of prescribed medications. He began drinking and lived life on the edge until he received his diagnosis of ALS. Rather than responding to this news with denial or resentment, he seemed to accept it. Grappling with the closeness of death, he stopped drinking, and his relationships began to transform.

One spring afternoon, when Uncle Bert was in late-stage ALS, we had a visit with him. I was a teenager at the time. Despite the gravity of his prognosis and the difficulty he now had in speaking, he lived in lightness, finding humour in unlikely places, laughing a lot and making us laugh too. On a trip to Las Vegas, he told us, he lost his bladder function in a hotel elevator and joked about it with the strangers who happened to be there with him. I would call my extended family emotionally conservative: while we are fairly close, we aren't openly affectionate, and we don't exchange those three little words. But as we were saying goodbye, Uncle Bert looked at me and said, "I love you." I gave a soft "I love you" in return, feeling a little out of my comfort zone, but meaning the words all the same. His simple statement has stayed with me over the years.

In the end, Uncle Bert told us that he wouldn't trade ALS for anything. The disease was a **wake-up call**, a gift that changed him. The way I see it, it helped him find his true self beneath the hurt that had engulfed his life. It opened him up to love, acceptance, and surrender—to life and everything in it—to true happiness. A few short years of happiness were worth more to him than a lifetime of misery. Uncle Bert is a major role model for me, though he will never know it.

My Wake-up Call

For me, too, the hardest moments in my life transformed me, catalyzing my search for a meaningful, peaceful, and joyful life. These challenges taught me to focus on not only my *life situation*, but *life* itself.

In my first pregnancy, I hoped for a natural delivery, so I got a midwife and took prenatal classes. These classes introduced me to pain management techniques, including meditation, visualizations, and breathing exercises. Little did I know, these techniques would not be useful to me during my labour and delivery, but they sure would be later on.

In the thirty-seventh week of my pregnancy, I got a tremendous headache that wouldn't go away. My husband, Todd, took me to the hospital to get checked out. My blood pressure had spiked dangerously high. I was placed into a dark room as my blood pressure continued to be monitored. Suddenly, I started convulsing and vomiting. Todd screamed for the nurse. I was having a seizure. It looked to Todd like I was dying.

And I might have. I had eclampsia, a serious pregnancy disorder characterized by seizures and risk of multi-organ failure. The nurses rushed me to the operating room, and Carter was born via emergency C-section. A couple days later, I suffered a postpartum seizure and ended up back in the ICU at the hospital. For a while I felt that my life was touch and go. In my darkest moments, I pictured myself giving in to what was happening to me, curled into a ball on a giant hand. It must have been the hand of God. *Let Go.*

With the help of anti-seizure medication, my condition was stabilized, and after almost two weeks in the hospital, I was discharged with a healthy baby boy.

Following my time in the hospital, I suffered post-traumatic anxiety. It mostly came on at night when I was lying in bed. My heart would start beating uncontrollably fast; it was hard to breathe. I felt restricted somehow, trapped by an unnameable fear.

I'd get up and lie back down, but no dice. Nothing was wrong with me, not physically anyhow. So why couldn't I breathe?

Remembering my prenatal classes, I tried the meditation and visualization techniques I'd been taught. Lying in bed, I focused on my breathing.

Breathe in.
Breathe out.
Breathe in.
Breathe out.

Sometimes I counted each breath to help keep me focused. Other times, I closed my eyes and imagined I was floating on a raft in the ocean, drifting peacefully, rising and falling with each gentle wave. My breath fell into the rhythm of the ebb and flow of each wave, slow and steady. I was safe. The panicky feeling would recede and I'd drift off to sleep. Eventually, these bouts of anxiety stopped coming on altogether.

That time of my life was my wake-up call. I realized how precarious life is, and how precious. My health could no longer be taken for granted. I felt deeply grateful for having been given the chance to keep on living.

If life were just a bed of roses, there would be limited opportunity for true growth. Researchers have found that difficult experiences, crises, and major stresses commonly lead to notable personal development—a phenomenon called "Adversarial Growth" or "Post-Traumatic Growth." It doesn't always work that way, though—all depends on mindset. The individual must accept the reality of the situation and perceive setbacks and challenges as opportunities if a new perspective is to be gained.[24]

As Stephen Covey suggests in *The 7 Habits of Highly Effective People*, I sometimes remind myself of my mortality to refresh my focus. What better way to determine if I am living my best life than picturing my life coming to an end? When I visualize myself at my own funeral or imagine that I have only a year left to live, it brings clarity to what I value most and how I want to spend my days. [25] And that's with inner peace and happiness! As writer Nanea Hoffman so eloquently puts it: "None of us are getting out of here alive, so please stop treating yourself like an afterthought. Eat the delicious food. Walk in the sunshine. Jump in the ocean. Say the truth that you're carrying in your heart like hidden treasure. Be silly. Be kind. Be weird. There's no time for anything else."[26]

When: The Present Moment

The Now is inseparable from who you are at the deepest level.

—Eckhart Tolle

It's all too easy for my daily routine to feel like a daily grind. Get up, get ready, drop the kids off, ride the train, attend meetings, work through lunch (the to-do list is too long to take a break!), attend more meetings, ride the train, pick up the kids, make dinner, eat dinner, help with homework, put the kids to bed, go to bed. Rinse, wash, repeat.

Sound familiar? Are we having fun yet?

If I'm not happy now, doing all of this, when will I be? Right smack in the middle of my busy life is the time to practise mindful awareness so that I can enjoy it as it's happening.

Time is an interesting concept. There's time as the calendar marks it, based on the earth's rotation around the sun. And then there's time in the way we perceive it. One day, my sister asked the rest of my family how we visualize a year. I think of it linearly, like the calendar, and so does my brother. But my mom and sister see time in a circular way. When I say "There isn't enough time in a day," this isn't an empirical measurement of the twenty-four-hour day, but a description of how my mind interacts with time. There's a discrepancy between the time it would take to accomplish all the tasks I expect to do in a day and the twenty-four hours that I actually have to work with. Often, it isn't physically possible for me to tick off all the boxes, leaving me disappointed. And my expectations of tasks I'll have achieved extend beyond my day to the upcoming week, month, and year—even my entire lifetime. With all these expectations come a lot of opportunities for disappointment.

But expectations are about the future. The future is a mental construct of a time that has not yet arrived. It exists only in my imagination. It is not real. I can't actually do anything in the future. And what about the past? A mental construct of time that lies behind me. I can't change it, and I certainly can't control it. It's gone. I can't do anything in the past— both the past and the future exist solely in my mind. The only real time that truly exists is the present moment. That is when and where mindful awareness takes place. As soon as I step outside of the present moment, I am experiencing events in my mind only. Any feelings that arise are triggered by the constructs of my mind.

To live in the present moment is to live my real life. Moments become days; days become years; years become a lifetime. It's uncanny to realize how much time I've spent fixated on past events or imagining the future. But I don't have to get caught up in either. I can focus on the very moment I'm in right now. Anyhow, this moment is the only time in which it's possible to take action. This is all I can control: my actions, in *this* moment.

Ideal Moments to Practise Mindful Awareness

Speaking of time, let's consider opportunities that are good times to practice mindfulness. When I notice that I have gotten lost in thought that is a good cue for me. As I noted earlier, strong emotions like anxiety, sadness, or anger are a useful marker. Nervousness tends to kick in before giving a presentation at work. I pause and ask myself what got me so stressed. The answer: I've been engaged in a negative thought pattern. *What if my presentation is boring? What if I forget what I am supposed to say?* Then I begin practising mindful awareness. I spend a moment to take a deep breath, feeling the air coming into and out of my body. I look out the window at the clouds high in the sky. I pay attention to others in the room with me and engage with them in a mindful way.

Mornings are another ideal time to practise. My mind feels fresh, not yet clouded by the craziness of the world around me. As the COVID-19 pandemic is currently ongoing, I have been working from home for the past few months. The time I would normally spend commuting, I dedicate to a mindful walk with Todd, followed by ten minutes of solo mindfulness practice. Sitting in the backyard on a yoga mat, I listen to the birds and watch the clouds roll by, or the patterns of light and shadow on the grass created by the sun's rays through the trees. Even a bit of time spent practising mindful awareness in the morning helps me start off my day with a positive mindset.

I also like to practise mindfulness when I'm waiting in line. Instead of pulling out my phone, which I do instinctively, I simply stand still and direct my attention to the sights and sounds around me. Or else, I practise during routine tasks such as washing my hands or doing the dishes. Rather than giving myself up to autopilot, I focus on the feeling of the warm water flowing over my hands.

Once, while I was practising mindfulness on the commuter train, I smiled at a lady sitting across from me. She smiled back and started talking to me. We had a very nice chat on our ride that day. That wonderful connection wouldn't have happened if I had been looking at my phone instead, disengaged from my surroundings.

But I don't need to wait for my morning commute, a work presentation, a lineup, or a chore to practise mindful awareness. Now is the time to practise, as there truly is no other time. Every moment is an opportunity to be happy.

How: Mindful Journaling

Every one of us already has the seed of mindfulness. The practice is to cultivate it.

—Thich Nhat Hanh

After years of letting my mind run wild, it was clear that it would take steady discipline to retrain it. I needed a solid mindfulness practice that I could commit to working into my daily routine to instill that discipline.

Ample research points to a strong connection between happiness, mindfulness, positivity, and gratitude. Writing is often advocated as a powerful technique to develop a positive outlook. A decade of empirical studies has proven that writing down positive things on a regular basis has a profound effect on the way our brains are wired. In one study, participants who wrote down three things that went well each day and their causes every night for a week were found to be happier and less depressed during their follow-ups over the next six months.[27] An article in the Journal of Clinical Psychology suggests, "Setting aside time on a daily basis to recall moments of gratitude associated with even mundane or ordinary events, personal attributes one has, or valued people one encounters has the potential to weave together a sustainable life theme of gratefulness just as it nourishes a fundamentally affirming life stance. . . . A number of evidence-based strategies, including journaling and letter writing, have proven effective in creating sustainable gratefulness."[28]

I was sold: daily journaling with a focus on mindfulness and gratitude. There was little to no downside to trying it out, and besides, who could argue with the research? I chose my morning train commute as the locus for my new practice.

I started each entry by observing my surroundings in mindful awareness, then jotting down what I noticed and any feelings that arose. Next, I wrote about whatever came to mind, often challenges that I was facing at home or at work. Finally, I invited myself to reflect on the situation from a mindful perspective. As time went on, I learned more about the benefits of gratitude, so I increased my focus on things I was grateful for.

I tried to write most days, but some weeks were more fruitful than others. On days that I didn't journal, I still engaged in a mindful awareness exercise: sitting in silence, noticing the sensations in my body and observing my surroundings. For close to three years, I kept up a regular journaling practice. By then, my mindset had shifted so much that the benefits were palpable. I was calmer, more patient and confident, both at home and at work. My relationships were deeper and I felt more connected to many people in my life. My overall sense of inner peace and happiness had improved immensely.

How to Use This Book

Through my process of mindful journaling, key themes emerged to form the elements of my formula for inner peace and happiness in daily life. First, there is the foundational element of *Presence*: living in the present moment. Also significant are *Gratitude, Purpose, Intention, Balance, Do Your Best, Let Go,* and last but not least, *Love*. At the end of each journal entry, I noted the most salient themes that came up for me on that day. They are discussed in more detail at the end of the book.

I encourage you to pause at the end of any journal entry that speaks to you and jot down your personal responses to the following:

- Have you experienced any similar challenges in your own life? Did similar feelings arise for you?
- Consider the themes listed at the end of the entry. Do any of them feel currently relevant in your life?
- List three things that you feel grateful for today.
- Perhaps write your own journal entry for the day.

Finally, give yourself a big hug. Experiment with feeling gratitude for investing time in yourself today and bringing attention to your own inner peace and happiness.

The joys of life can be found in the everyday moments. We just have to be awake to experience them.

Waking Up: The Journal

Life moves pretty fast. If you don't stop and look around once in a while, you could miss it.

—Ferris Bueller, *Ferris Bueller's Day Off*

Tuesday, January 6, 2015 – First entry

It's 7:10 am. Our train just left the local station to take us to Union Station in downtown Toronto. I'm sitting next to my husband, Todd, with our coffees in our travel mugs. He's already on his tablet reading about IT system administration. It's so dark outside; all I can see when I look out of the GO train window is a reflection of me and my fellow early morning commuters.

Todd and I have been married for twelve and a half years now. We met and dated in high school, and after going our separate ways for a while, we reconnected after our university years. We had done some growing and maturing through those years and were better positioned to be in a long-term relationship. Now, here we are, happily married and commuting together daily to our jobs in the city.

Todd started his career as a Bay Street lawyer. I often say he's one of the smartest people I know. He scored in the 98th percentile on his Law School Admission Test (LSAT). But he's very modest and would never mention that to anyone (and won't be happy about my saying it here). He started out doing corporate law and then switched to tax law. After a few years, he realized that the life of a corporate lawyer with the long, unforgiving hours wasn't fulfilling for him. He joined the in-house legal services team at an accounting firm for a few years, then settled into a department at the provincial government focusing on corporate tax design, which is where he is now. He's reasonably happy with his current role. It offers intellectual challenges, which is important to him, along with regular working hours, which allows for a good work-life balance.

Since we both commute to the city, we're away from the house about eleven hours every day. We hired a full-time nanny to alleviate our worries about being away from the boys for such long hours. We also wanted to make our daily routines less hectic. Carter, our firstborn son, is now seven years old. His younger brother, Austin, is four and a half.

Austin had a high fever through the night. Thankfully, his temperature went down with Tylenol and he was still sleeping when we left. I may come home early today if it goes back up. Lolita, our nanny, will keep me posted through the morning. In terms of my calendar, today doesn't look too bad, but my to-do list is as long as always. There's an executive briefing tomorrow that I'm scheduled to present at, so preparation will occupy my time today.

A cold, dark January morning doesn't naturally lift the spirits so I'll look to other things . . . Carter's sweet voice calling up from the basement to say "Goodbye, I love you" as we left the house . . . the warmth and closeness of Todd sitting next to me . . . a fresh coffee and homemade breakfast shake in my bag that Todd made this morning . . . the cuddles I had with Austin at three o'clock in the morning as I stroked his warm face before he drifted back to sleep.

Love. Presence. Gratitude.

Wednesday, January 7 – It takes a village

Another dark, cold January morning. Right now it's -15°C, and it feels like -26°C with the wind chill. A cold that freezes your nostrils as you breathe in.

Austin seemed to be getting better yesterday, but his fever spiked in the middle of the night again. Poor little guy. It's stressful enough when one of the boys is sick, but today is an extra stressful time as Todd and I both have meetings where we're doing presentations. Hopefully Austin is better this morning, but in the meantime I'm thinking through alternatives to get him to the doctor if he needs to, as Lolita doesn't drive. My mom? My sister?

I come from a pretty big family, as my dad is one of five kids and my mom is one of six. I'm the second-oldest of four. There's my older sister, Heather (married to Richard with three children), my younger sister, Janice (we call her Jai, married to Steve with a daughter), and my younger brother, Stu. My parents still live in the rural farmhouse where my siblings and I grew up. The property and house have been in my family since the 1800s, when my dad's great-grandfather settled in Canada from England.

Since we lived in the country growing up, a car ride away from any friends, my siblings and I became each others' closest friends and playmates. Whether it was riding bikes, playing in the creek, skipping with our jump ropes, or playing with Barbie dolls, we relied on each other for companionship. This closeness has stuck through the years. They form part of my "village" of support. As the saying goes, it takes a village to raise a child.

As we broaden the definition of the village, the more powerful the concept becomes. We are all connected. If we go back millennia and millennia, at some point, we are all related to one another. We are all on this journey, on this planet together. We don't have to feel so separate, disconnected, or competitive with one another.

I think about Carter and Austin and the sports teams they're on. As a parent watching their baseball games, I find myself so fixated on my sons and their teams. Cheering them on, hoping for the win, because isn't that the main goal here? I easily get swept away in the competition and how well we're doing, barely noticing the other five-year-olds that are playing their little hearts out on the other team. They're showing up and working hard. Why don't I recognize that more and give them a big "Way to go, little guy"? The different jersey colour has made such an impact on my mindset: they're the "other" team against ours. But really, they're sweet little boys and girls, doing their best and improving their skills, just like mine are. Here is another great opportunity to practise mindful awareness: watching sports. Rather than identifying only with one team, I can try for a degree of objectivity and celebrate both.

As a parent, I tend to think of my children as "mine" and thus, other children as "belonging" to someone else. But after reading *The Conscious Parent* by Dr. Shefali Tsabary,[29] I have a slightly different perspective. My children are those that I'm fortunate enough to have come into my life, that I have the privilege of guiding. They are not "mine" to control. They are their own people with their own unique talents, desires, and personalities. Of course, they still need structure and support, and that's a big part of parenting.

What if I took on the broad village view? What if I saw all children (and people in general for that matter) as part of a single community? No matter where they come from, healthy, happy individuals benefit everyone around them.

That reminds me of Albert Einstein's view on widening circles:

> A human being is a part of the whole called by us the "Universe," a part limited in time and space. He experiences

himself, his thoughts and feeling as something separated from the rest—a kind of optical delusion of his consciousness. This delusion is a kind of prison for us, restricting us to our personal desires and to affection for a few persons nearest to us. Our task must be to free ourselves from this prison by **widening our circle of compassion to embrace all living creatures** and the whole of nature in its beauty.[30]

What a big village we actually have when we consider this perspective.

Hopefully, Carter will be able to walk to the bus stop with his friend Richard while Lolita takes care of Austin. Community, family, and friends are so important! I'm grateful for them today.

Balance. Gratitude. Love.

Thursday, January 8 – *Lean In*

Another day, another sick boy. Happily, Austin improved a lot yesterday and was full of energy by the end of the day; however, Carter went to bed with a fever. I am so thankful for Lolita. She will stay home with both of them today. It's still very cold outside, so we thought another day of rest for Austin will be good.

I'm feeling a little less stressed today, as I got through the four-hour executive briefing yesterday. My presentation went well. Now back to focusing on the bank-specific work in my portfolio and trying to figure out a replacement for the manager who recently left my group, among other things on my to-do list. I am realizing that HR-related matters take up a lot of time in this new leadership role.

Recently, I received a promotion within my organization. It's been an adjustment being in an oversight role, as I was so used to being a "doer." As it is an executive-level position, leadership is a key component. The focus is more on setting directions and providing coaching for the staff and less on carrying out the tasks. I enjoy doing those tasks, so it will take a conscious effort to change gears. I now have three direct reports and a team of nine, and oversee a portfolio of around twenty-five banks and trust companies. I'm still figuring out expectations and the balance of my involvement without getting into the weeds. I am quite loyal and dedicated to my career (I've been with the organization for around thirteen years). I love the actual work and contributing in a positive way to Canada's financial services industry.

My family is also very important to me. I consider raising responsible and confident human beings as an extremely meaningful role. As Sheryl Sandberg discusses in her book, *Lean In: Women, Work, and the Will to Lead*,[31] I feel I can *lean in* to my career without sacrificing my commitments to my family. She suggests that many of us, women especially, hold ourselves back because we're worried we can't manage it all, parenting and career. Rather than stay in our comfort zones, she advises that we lean in and give it a try. We may just surprise ourselves and excel. Our careers can be part of a very fulfilling aspect of our lives, so we shouldn't underestimate our ability to find solutions and make the balance work. I've found that as I move *up* in the organization, I have *more* control over my schedule, and that flexibility benefits my work-life balance. And if I am fulfilled in my job, I might end up also being a better mother.

I'm motivated to perform both roles well—mother and leader. I will do my best and take it one day at a time.

Do Your Best. Balance. Presence. Gratitude.

Friday, January 9 – Swimming against the current

I'm not going to lie, it's Friday and the stress has crept in, as much as I try to keep it at bay. To be honest, it feels like a real struggle, like I'm swimming against the current to maintain a balanced life and not get caught up in the work frenzy. Urgent demands keep coming at me from every direction: staff, fellow directors, the managing director, colleagues in other departments, etc., each focusing on their own agenda. As the week goes by, I find the pressure mounting, which makes it harder for me to stay mindful and present.

I'm trying to forget an unfortunate discussion I had with my boss yesterday where I was trying to express some concerns and stresses in our group. What he said to me actually made me feel much worse. For every comment I made, he had a rebuttal. He didn't seem to be truly listening. When he made a comment about expectations for overtime in a professional organization where everyone makes a certain amount of money, it gave me pause. I have to wonder, to what end? Are we being paid for the number of hours we spend in the office or the quality of the work we produce? What's more important, input or output?

Back when I worked at an accounting firm, we were sometimes expected to stay at the client's office very late, even after we had completed our work for the day, just to put in what we called "face time" (not to be confused with the Apple FaceTime app; that didn't exist yet). It bothered me so much because I'm a results-oriented person. I want to be adding value in everything I do, and face time didn't feel like it added any value at all. I wonder if this overtime-for-the-sake-of-overtime is a larger societal issue or if it's specific to my own industry.

In the age of information, it seems that everything is more, more, more. Even though we now have more access to information and more digital technology, it hasn't actually made our jobs any easier or more efficient—it has just increased expectations for productivity. Back in the day when accounting was paper-based T accounts and everything was done manually, we could only dream that our jobs be done in half the time. Think of all the extra time we'd have to do things we enjoyed: spend time with our families, take care of our community. . . . What happened to that dream? The saved time just got replaced with more work, and we're working harder than ever. Has our society gotten to a better place because of it?

When I step back and look at the big picture, it's hard to say whether we're moving forward. I've been bringing awareness to my goals and how they map to the busyness of modern society. Hopefully, it'll help me make intentional choices and challenge the status quo where it's warranted.

This is my opportunity to pause. To look out the window of the train and think about what a blessing this day is. I have to strain to see past the reflections in the glass. When I do, I see early signs of dawn. I see the darkness falling away, snow-covered roofs, a few lights on in the houses, a few cars on the road. It looks quiet and peaceful.

Let Go. Presence. Gratitude.

Tuesday, January 13 – Dark days: the lull

After spending a few days working from home, tending to Carter as he got better, here I am again, back on the early morning GO train platform. Revelling in the fresh albeit cold air (-31°C) while I wait for the train. Marvelling at the clear indigo sky with a perfect crescent moon hanging high above.

I'm actually kind of looking forward to getting back to my usual routine at the office today after being at home all weekend with cancelled plans and a sick boy. I enjoyed the time with the family, cuddling with the boys, watching Downton Abbey with Todd, reading *House in the Sky*. But I do crave social interactions after a quiet time like that.

I also feel the need to get out for a walk today. I feel the pull of the dark January days, lulling me into sedentary hibernation mode. Todd and I have been doing a daily seven-minute HIIT workout (High Intensity Interval Training) through an app. The sequence of exercises is scientifically proven to promote weight loss and improve cardiovascular function. Apart from that workout, though, exercise has been limited.

It takes extra effort—or perhaps just acceptance, depending on how you look at it—to stay present and grateful during the lull of these short, dark days. Studies show a potential correlation between weather and mood, and I can only imagine that in Canada, depression levels must be highest in mid-January, when the energy and excitement of the December holiday season has worn off.

This poem by a Zen master reminds me that outer circumstances like the current season don't need to dictate my happiness:

> *Ten thousand flowers in spring, the moon in autumn,*
> *a cool breeze in summer, snow in winter.*
> *If your mind isn't clouded by unnecessary things,*
> *this is the best season of your life.*
>
> —Wumen Huikai

Stay conscious. I must give myself regular reminders.

Presence. Balance.

Wednesday, January 14 – Balance: the yin and yang

Another cold, dark January morning. I can see a subtle strip of orange low on the horizon as the sun prepares to emerge.

Todd sits next to me with his coffee and tablet, reading about Unix. Computer stuff. He has a technical mind that thrives on facts and figures and a thirst for knowledge that I find impressive. Although in some ways, our minds work very differently, I think we make a good match. He and I both have practical, analytical minds, but I have a strong intuitive side as well. As with other aspects of our personalities (he's an introvert and I'm an extrovert), we balance each other out. His yin to my yang.

I appreciate it more now, after many years of marriage, but these differences caused tensions earlier on in our relationship. I was always, and I mean *always* up for going out with friends, attending a party, or visiting family members. He wasn't always enthusiastic about the idea and often preferred a quiet evening at home. It was a challenge: on the one hand, I craved social interaction, but on the other, I wanted to spend time with him.

This was actually the main cause of our breakup in high school. Todd is three years older than me, so when we started dating in high school, I was in grade 10 and he was in his final year. He'd already spent four years partying; I was just getting started. When the weekend rolled around, I wanted to go out with friends while he was happier with a movie or dinner date. I wasn't ready to sacrifice my social life for a relationship so we ended up breaking up, as sad as I was, because in my heart I really loved him.

Even in our marriage, our extrovert/introvert differences have led to many disagreements, mainly on the weekends. We've found a bit of a groove now. I've become more independent in socializing, so I'll go out with friends without him. The big change is really in our mindsets and our appreciation of each others' needs. We removed expectations we had of each other and our relationship. My own expectation was *couples should go to social gatherings together*. I don't feel as bad when he doesn't attend an event with me anymore, as I understand that it isn't personal. He also makes an effort to venture out of his comfort zone and go out on the weekends. It's all about balance.

I'm grateful for our partnership and marriage, how we continue to learn from each other and balance one another.

Let Go. Balance. Presence.

Thursday, January 15 – Health and death

I'm feeling especially grateful for my health today. I never want to take it for granted. I had some blood work done and I misinterpreted the message from my doctor about following up with her. I wasn't aware that I was stressing about it in the back of my mind, imagining all the possibilities of what could be wrong with me. When I saw her yesterday and she confirmed that the blood work all looked normal, a huge wave of relief washed over me. Interesting, though: my worry was about the impact a sick or dying mother would have on her children, not about myself. I recently read a good article by Deepak Chopra about the importance of self-care and not waiting until there is a problem, because by then it may be too late. To borrow the language of risk management from my job, I should be *proactive* rather than *reactive* with my health.

This is another reminder for me to live in the moment, exercise regularly, make healthy food choices, and prioritize what's most important to me. I shouldn't neglect my health or my loved ones. So often, I get caught up in work tasks and chores, failing to focus on what really matters. After all, I've only got one life to live before I die.

It's interesting to contemplate my fear of death. What about it is so scary? I guess I have certain expectations about life and death: *I should have a long life; I shouldn't suffer; death shouldn't happen suddenly.* But it might be the uncertainty around death that I'm most uncomfortable with. It's something I can't control. I don't know when I'll die. I don't know how. I don't know what will happen after I die. I somewhat believe in a kind of afterlife or reincarnation of the spirit, but obviously, I can't know for sure.

So instead, I push this reality aside and concentrate on the day-to-day. I cling to the things I *can* control to maintain the illusion of total control. But the unknown is always just a whisper away.

Imagine I learned to confront my fear of death. What if I were to live in complete acceptance of death? What would that look like? And since I'm destined to die, is there anything I would change about the way I'm living my life?

I'm thinking: instill independence, confidence, and love in my children so that they'll be okay if I'm no longer physically in the world with them.

Purpose. Presence. Gratitude. Let Go.

Friday, January 16 – Life is a marathon, not a sprint

It's Friday. Looking back on the week, it hasn't been too bad. After getting my presentation out of the way, I focused on the core work in my portfolio, along with coaching my staff. It's been a hectic transition, being thrown into this new role while juggling my old one until my boss finds a successor. I love to be challenged, and this is one of those opportunities. I must admit, though, it's not a comfortable feeling, and sometimes I'm hard on myself. I have a lot of new files to learn, and I don't like the feeling of not knowing everything about the banks. My intention is to focus on doing my best each day, knowing that I won't be perfect and that I'm learning as I go.

As part of a succession planning exercise, my boss asked me how long I've been with the organization and when I might expect to retire. It's crazy to think that I've been here for over twelve years and in the workforce for fifteen. If I retire at sixty years old, it'll be 2037. That's twenty-three years away. Twenty-three years, forty hours per week, fifty-two weeks per year: that makes 47,840 hours in total. I'd certainly better enjoy what I'm doing at work!

I should give myself a break in terms of expectations. I still have a lot of time to learn all that my new role entails. As my boss has said, think of your career as a marathon, not a sprint. I think this is good advice. We're more likely to experience burnout and other repercussions on our mental and physical health if we approach life as a sprint. That is one long sprint. I mean, hopefully a long one.

Presence. Intention. Do Your Best. Let Go.

Monday, January 19 – Friendships for the soul

It's a much milder morning than it has been, a balmy -1°C. I'm feeling somewhat refreshed after the weekend. While Saturday was a pretty crazy day with all our activities, it ended wonderfully with some quality time with my girlfriends. I'm so fortunate to have a great group of friends who have stuck together over the years. The group is like a snowball that has rolled through time, getting bigger along the way. It started with my childhood friend Janis and me. The snowball grew in high school, gathering Kelly, Julie, and Shannon. When we left for university, Janis to Toronto and I to London, the snowball continued rolling: Kate and Kristin from Janis' residence; Marnie, Nicole, and Amy, my roommates at school. Janis, Kate, and I became roommates in Toronto after we graduated. Later on, the three of us plus Nicole all settled in the same town, and it's wonderful for our kids to be able to grow up together. Carter and Austin call my friends' kids "cousins" since they feel like part of our extended family.

All my girlfriends have grown close over the years, accompanying each other through various stages of life. We celebrated our weddings together, the births of our children, tonnes of birthdays, and the more difficult times—the deaths of family members, divorces, illnesses, and other challenges we inevitably face. These are the events that connect us. We see each other at our best and also at our most vulnerable, and embrace each other in all our imperfections.

Seeing my friends experience hardships makes me realize that no one is without challenges in life. Like them, I am a human being, doing the best I can. They help me be a little more comfortable with that.

I have deep friendships within my family as well. My sisters and brother are my closest friends and confidantes. We grew up with my mom's cousin Eileen's family side by side, so my second cousins Emily and Laura also feel like sisters of mine. It was Emily who first introduced me to meditation. A CD she gave me got me through my post-traumatic anxiety from the pregnancy seizures. We continue to support each other as we go through life's various challenges.

I'm thankful that the boys have good friends at school too. I was just commenting to Todd that it feels like I have a part-time side gig as Carter's social coordinator, managing and setting up his playdates. Austin also seems to just love all his friends at school. When he listed off the friends he wanted to have over for his birthday party, he named his entire class. There wasn't one classmate he didn't want to invite.

On Saturday night after Kate's daughter's birthday party, a group of us sat around, having wine and chatting. Kristin and Janis are both pregnant with their third child, and their husbands were trying to convince everyone else to have three kids too. Ha! Having a child is definitely not something I want to do because of peer pressure!

Quality time with good friends is food for the soul. Numerous studies show how important social connections are to happiness. Some psychologists describe social bonds as being a biological need, as essential as air, food, and water in humans' well-being.[32]

I'm very grateful for all our friendships. I will be mindful to continue to cultivate my relationships and be thankful for them every day.

Love. Balance. Do Your Best. Gratitude.

Wednesday, January 21 – The power of education

I gaze out the window of the train. It seems to be a fraction lighter this morning. The days are ever-so-slowly getting longer. I admire the elegance of the Toronto skyline, streaked with pink and blue just above the horizon. Beautiful.

Austin was upset last night as he told us about his day. A classmate decided it would be funny to push him in the snow. Everyone laughed except one boy named Ashton. Because it entertained the others, the classmate kept pushing him during both recesses. We had a family discussion about ideas for dealing with bullying behaviour. Carter shared the S.T.O.P. method that he's been taught at school: Speak up, Tell an adult, Our solution, Positive. Austin replied that he did speak up, telling the boy to stop and that he wouldn't be his friend if he kept doing stuff like that. Todd and I told him we were proud of the way he'd handled it. We also commented on how good it was of Ashton not to laugh and encourage the bad behaviour of the other boy.

The challenges that my children face are definitely hard to hear about, but they're also good learning opportunities. Because, sadly, there are bullies in the adult world too. The behaviour may present itself differently than pushing folks in the snow, but it can be just as harmful and perhaps more so, if we let it continue.

We watched some inspirational videos on YouTube about a teenager who was getting bullied a lot. He started holding the doors open for his classmates, and that simple act of kindness gained him a positive reputation among his classmates and turned his life around. Carter really enjoyed it and asked to watch it again. He'd held a door open for people yesterday and felt quite proud.

Both boys have had excellent teachers every year so far. Austin's kindergarten class recently read the book *Have You Filled a Bucket Today? A Guide to Daily Happiness for Kids* by Carol McCloud. Since then, they've been talking about "filling each other's buckets." They also do yoga and dance a lot in class. Austin has been showing us his "Shake it off" moves around the house. It's so great that they are teaching kindness and happiness in school. **Empathy, emotional intelligence, and happiness are such important factors for success in life.** They really should be included in schools' core curriculums.

> *Education is the most powerful weapon you can use to change the world.*
>
> —Nelson Mandela

Presence. Intention. Love. Gratitude.

Thursday, January 22 – The burning log

The week seems to get busier as it goes on. Today, I have three back-to-back meetings with three different banks, along with a retirement celebration for a colleague. I'm noticing again that toward the end of the week, work is more likely to be consuming my thoughts, and living in the moment becomes more of a challenge.

I think mindfulness begets mindfulness, and conversely, living on autopilot begets more of the same. I've heard an analogy of a burning log: if you place a burning log next to another burning log, both flames become stronger. But if you place a burning log next to a cold log, depending on how robust the flame is, the cold log may extinguish it. Similarly, if we're surrounded by people who are living mindfully, it's easier to follow suit, and we're less likely to slip into unhealthy thought patterns.

So many people around me in the train are commuting to downtown Toronto to work in corporate environments where formidable egos reign. Many of us must be walking around with egos unchecked. Now that I'm igniting a "fire" of mindful awareness inside myself, I'd better be a pretty hot log if I want to keep that fire burning.

With so many people crossing each others' paths in the city, it's funny how rare it is to see them smile at each other. Those who do are almost always previously acquainted. It seems awkward to smile at a stranger because it's so uncommon, but I'd like to make a conscious effort to do it more anyhow, including to the homeless people I walk by. Smiling isn't a difficult thing to do, and it can lead to a ripple effect of positivity. I want to be a burning log for others.

Presence. Intention.

Monday, January 26 – *The Conscious Parent*

A surprise snowfall last night has made for a brighter commute this morning thanks to the blanket of white surrounding us. The sun is also up as we're on a later train, having taken extra time to shovel the driveway.

Carter challenged my sense of inner peace on Saturday when he refused to go onto the ice for his hockey class. The accountant in me knew that every second of his not being on the ice was wasted money. Thinking about how much I'd paid for the class, I struggled to keep my rising anger at bay. He'd taken hockey lessons last session and enjoyed them, so I wasn't sure what the problem was. I didn't want to force him onto the ice, though I knew that once he got out there he would be fine. But I also didn't want him to think that he could just walk away from commitments at whim. I tried to encourage him and reason with him. No luck. *Grrr.*

Stay calm.

I decided to try my hand at channelling the lessons I'd learned from Dr. Shefali Tsabary's book *The Conscious Parent*. **I took my attention away from my own thoughts and focused on him and what his needs were in that moment.**[33] What was causing him this anxiety?

Finally, as we talked it over, I started to understand what was going on in his mind. They had put him in a new group on a new rink. He didn't like changing groups or moving away from the rink he was used to from the last session with his friend Ben. So we talked to the instructors and asked if he could switch back to his old group. Problem solved. Crisis averted. He got onto the ice right away and even scored two goals during his class, which made him extra happy. Wow, does it ever pay to be a Conscious Parent! I will have to try this more often.

A busy week lies ahead of me, so I'll have to take it moment by moment.

Presence. Let Go.

Tuesday, February 3 – The disease of busyness

We had a nice weekend with our usual Saturday activities (the kids' skating, hockey, and breakdance classes) along with a birthday party for Jeffrey, my friend Janis' son.

Since our Saturday schedule is generally very packed, we've designated Sunday as our day to unwind. We try not to plan anything and create space for ourselves. It is just as important, if not more, than the activities. The boys are in their glory when they have a full day to play at home. I, on the other hand, tend to get antsy. I'm used to having all my time pre-arranged and accounted for. But since our nanny, Lolita, has been with us, there's been more free time for Todd and I on the weekends, as she does the laundry and cleaning through the week. I have an odd urge to fill up all that time.

Social media is full of ideas for things to do, with so many posts of fun activities people are doing. FOMO (fear of missing out) kicks in. So I started my day looking into where I could go for a yoga class or pedicure. But we were expecting a snowstorm, so I was hesitant to go out. I decided to create a relaxing day for myself at home. It started with a workout (seven-minute HIIT with Todd, forty-five minutes on the elliptical), followed by a DIY spa (bubble bath, candles, yoga playlist, facial, pedicure). It was so lovely and I didn't have to leave the house or spend a dime. Hmm, I think I can get used to having spare time in my schedule.

Why is it that we feel compelled to be constantly "doing" things? I shared an article on Facebook a few weeks ago called "The Disease of Busyness" that describes this phenomenon. I think a lot of us have it, motoring through life with "busy" as our default setting, always getting ready for the next thing. But time out is good for everyone. After all, **we are human beings, not human doings.** We still have value when we aren't in the middle of doing something.

That said, yesterday was a productive day. I worked from home due to the snowstorm. Today is going to be very busy, full of meetings and negotiations with colleagues in other departments. Hopefully the quiet time from the weekend will help me stay more present amongst the busyness.

Presence. Intention. Balance.

Thursday, February 5 – Perspective

A little girl named Savannah passed away yesterday. I've been following her mom's blog about her fight with neuroblastoma, a type of cancer. She was diagnosed when she was two years old, and will now be "forever five." It's simply heartbreaking to think of the battle she and her family faced, the difficult decisions her mom had to make, because there is neither a cure nor a simple treatment.

It puts things in perspective: the way life unfolds, what little control we have on a fundamental level. These are the life situations that we can't control. I really should learn to flow with life, as fighting it will only result in stress and frustration. **All I can do is accept what is and appreciate all that is good and beautiful in the world in the moment that I'm in.** I can't change the past and I can't control the future. My perspective shapes my life. I can choose to fear the unknown and try to protect and control everything I can, or I can choose to surrender to the unknown and go with the flow, affecting what I can but accepting that I can't direct the vast majority of events. Accept. Enjoy. Trust. Flow.

I cherished the hugs and kisses and warm bodies in my bed with me this morning, perhaps a little more than usual. I sent out a prayer to Savannah's family for God to be with them and hold them close during this difficult time.

Let Go. Love. Gratitude.

Friday, February 6 – Positive reinforcement

Another cold day.

I took the day off yesterday so I could take the boys to their doctor's appointments. Carter had his annual checkup, and Austin had a speech therapy appointment with his "talking doctor."

We had a really nice evening doing a fun drawing activity recommended by Austin's speech therapist. Austin has what we call "bumpy" speech (aka stutter) at the beginning of certain words and sentences. It has been improving thanks to the home exercises. During the drawing activity, we praise him every time his speech is smooth, and after a minimum of four praises, we ask him to try a sentence again if it was bumpy. I find this to be such a good use of positive reinforcement—rather than focusing on the negative, we place attention on what our child is doing well.

This technique can be applied in other parenting situations, too. In *The Conscious Parent,* Dr. Shefali outlines an extreme example of emphasizing praise and reinforcing desired behaviour: A child was painting on a piece of paper taped to the wall. A lot of paint ended up on the wall itself. When the parent walked in, rather than commenting on the paint all over the wall, she praised the child for painting so beautifully on the paper. The child beamed and continued painting, making sure to stay on the paper. There were no hard feelings and the positive behaviour was reinforced.

So many parenting lessons apply to other life situations, as dealing with children is essentially dealing with people, just smaller ones. I can use positive reinforcement at work by showing appreciation for my staff members and giving them credit when they do something well. It can be beneficial in romantic relationships as well. I'll try it the next time I feel annoyed with Todd: I'll think of three things I appreciate about him and tell them to him first before I criticize something he did.

Presence. Love. Intention.

Monday, February 9 – Spirituality

It's brighter than usual outside the train this morning, mainly because it was delayed. We had a heavy snowfall over the weekend.

Our weekends are a little less busy these days, as Sunday mornings no longer involve going to church. Todd and I joined a community church when we moved to the neighbourhood around twelve years ago. But when major discord arose in the congregation, we reconsidered our membership and stopped attending.

I grew up going to a small Presbyterian church as a child, and I wanted my children to have a similar experience. There's value in taking time out of day-to-day life to consider the bigger picture. I had a lot of questions growing up about details of the Bible, and to be honest, I was never completely satisfied with the answers I was given. Regardless, it felt good sitting in the church pew on Sunday mornings, singing songs in harmony with the other parishioners and hearing stories of love, peace, and joy. There was something comforting in that simple Sunday morning routine that I shared with my family.

Even though Todd didn't grow up in a religious household and is somewhat skeptical of religion, when we first moved to town, we decided as a family to join a church. We attended services at a few different churches before landing on one that we really liked. It was very welcoming (after our first service a church member came by our house and dropped off a package of fair trade coffee), with a nice choir and a good children's program. I became quite active in Sunday school, taking turns leading the activities with my sister Heather and other parents with young children. It was a great group of people.

Unfortunately, other folks in the congregation were dissatisfied with the performance of the minister and wanted him replaced. The minister addressed the concerns raised in a number of congregational meetings, and a referendum was held: Stay or Leave. The congregation was pretty evenly split, but Leave won by a few votes. Throughout the meetings I witnessed behaviour that was so out of line with the teachings of Jesus Christ, notably of love and forgiveness. I found it hard to continue attending. A lot of our Sunday school subgroup felt the same way, so we sadly decided to move on from the community that had given us a sense of belonging for so many years.

It was an eye-opening experience. Religious organizations are organizations like any other: full of people. Imperfect people.

Spirituality is still very important to me. Recently, I've been exploring less conventional avenues: I read spiritual texts and spend time in nature. I also try to keep the spirit of God in my conversations with the boys. We say prayers of gratitude and have discussions about all of us being God's children and treating each other with love and kindness. That may be enough, but I'm not sure. I suppose this is part of our journey, and we'll keep our eyes open for bigger commitments on the spiritual front. Since I was raised a Christian, I use the term "God" and refer to Jesus, but I'm very open to other forms of religion. Meditation, yoga, and mindfulness all come from Eastern religions and philosophies. I believe all religions point to the same essence. Spirituality means recognizing that **we are more than just individuals; we're part of something greater, something connected.** It's the underpinning for everything else in our lives, so we need to nourish it in some form.

Purpose. Balance. Love. Intention. Gratitude.

Thursday, February 12 – Empowering decisions

I had a wonderful day yesterday. I took time off to volunteer at Carter's school's winter carnival. It was surprisingly productive as well. Austin and I had doctor's appointments later in the afternoon, and I sat with the boys as they worked on Valentine's Day cards.

I'm glad I made a conscious decision to spend time with my son and help out in our community. I very easily could have decided to go to work and attend to my to-do list. But in the end, making a decision based on my core values led to a super-productive day from a work perspective as well, without any guilt or regrets. It felt very empowering to take control and make a decision like this—win/win/win. A win for me, a win for my family, a win for my work.

I'm going to practise making more empowered decisions in my day. Decisions that are right for me holistically, even if they come up against the old-school mentality of my nine-to-five corporate-type office job. The flexibility of working from home is still much more of an anomaly than the rule at my office, despite the productivity that can be gained from it. Perhaps someday this will change.

Intention. Balance.

Friday, February 13 – Friday the 13th, need I say more?

It's an especially cold morning at -30°C, including the wind chill. *Brrr.* The boys were going to have a playdate with friends, but the walk to their house would be too cold and Lolita doesn't drive.

Todd, Austin, and I are fighting colds and we're all a little grumpy. Todd and I got into an argument on our way to the GO train. I guess I came across as trying to prove him wrong on a few things and I sounded self-righteous in our disagreement. He stormed away from me in the GO train parking lot.

I'm aware that this is one of my personality traits: I can sound preachy. I certainly don't think I'm better than anyone. I do like to help people, and if I know something that can be useful to them, I point it out. Unfortunately, there's a risk of seeming a little too helpful in my approach.

I have a vivid memory from university when I first became aware of this. My good friend Nicole and I were having a heart-to-heart and I gave her unsolicited relationship advice. She snapped at me, calling me self-righteous. It stung. I knew she was right, and indeed, that's how I sounded. I'm thankful for good friends who are honest and tell me the truth even if it's difficult to hear. This kind of friendship is priceless. It helps me truly grow as a person.

My goal is to listen more and give advice only when it's asked for. Also, I can give it in a more tentative way. Twenty years later and still working on this!

Todd and I don't usually stay mad at each other for long, so we're back to talking. Hmm, what's going on today? It's Friday and usually I'm a little more cheerful on a Friday.

Presence. Do Your Best. Balance. Gratitude.

Tuesday, February 17 – Creativity

It's yet another extremely cold day after a cold weekend of -30°C temperatures. The sky is slowly getting brighter and the sun has risen above the horizon, a big bright orange fireball.

Valentine's Day was on Saturday and Family Day was yesterday, so it made for a nice long weekend. I made Valentine's Day cards for Todd, Carter, and Austin. Todd's card read, "My heart has never known a greater joy than loving you." Carter and Austin's cards read, "You are the light of my life." I painted the cards and everything. Something feels so good about using those same creative skills I did as a kid, getting out the paints, crayons, markers, scissors, and glue. It's food for the soul.

I love my friend Natalie Davison's Master Mindset talk on creativity. She says: "Every human on this planet possesses it, but fifty percent of you are going to say, 'Oh, that's not me.' It's essential to our survival as a species and any growth or development that will occur on this earth, and yet half of you are not going to use that word."[34] She says that creativity is the stuff that comes from our soul. It's often reduced to activities like painting, crafts, music, etc. But creativity comes in many different forms and the definition she uses is "transcending traditional ideas and enacting new ideas." Natalie argues that we all need to tap into our creativity. If we don't, there will be a void that we'll try to fill in different ways, likely unhealthy. If we're struggling to realize our natural creativity, she suggests asking ourselves what we did as kids.

For me, as a child I loved playing sports, dancing (I used to do a Mickey Mouse Jazzercise routine), playing business lady and teacher, writing (I kept a journal as a child, which is hilarious to read now), and doing made-up projects similar to those I did at school. For example, one lonely summer in the countryside, I researched birds and pasted the information and pictures I'd compiled onto a large piece of Bristol board.

Creativity feels good because it's a way to pause and reconnect with myself. It's similar to mindful awareness in that way. Just like when I quiet my mind, as I pull out the scissors and glue, I become more connected. And in that stillness, new ideas emerge. I can solve a problem I've been struggling with for hours when I tune in to that quiet state.

Presence. Do Your Best. Balance.

Wednesday, February 18 – Technology Addictions

This morning did not go smoothly. Carter was crying, protesting that he didn't want to go to school. I spent time with him trying to understand why. I think it's because he would rather spend the day on the computer. It's been a challenge getting him off the computer once he gets on. Todd thinks that it's great that he's interested in the computer just like his dad, especially if he's doing programming or playing creative building games (like Minecraft). But he seems obsessed with it. To me it doesn't seem healthy.

It's not just kids who are struggling with the overuse of technology. I have to be mindful of the time I spend on my phone and computer too. There are so many apps that pull me in for prolonged periods of time. They are literally designed to be addictive. There's the infinite scroll on news and social media sites. It's amazing how I go to check something specific on Facebook, and an hour later I know what my neighbour had for dinner, I've seen a myriad of pictures of friends on outings that make me feel like my life is boring, and I've succumbed to some mommies' chat group drama about whether a participant should stay with her cheating husband. Of course she shouldn't—oops, this wasn't the plan. Seriously, how did I end up reading that thread and where did that time go? If I had made a conscious choice, I almost certainly would have chosen to spend my precious time doing something else.

Another reason to stay mindful in the face of social influences and technology.

Intention. Presence.

Friday, February 20 – Mistakes and time-outs

It was a rough morning. I woke up late and wasn't feeling well, as I'm coming down with a cold. I felt grumpy and impatient last night too, notably at bedtime. I actually gave myself a time-out after I yelled at the boys when they came up to bed complaining about being hungry. They had left the dinner table to play on the computer, evidently before they were full.

The computer was the star of the morning too, as Carter went straight to it before eating breakfast or getting dressed. Since there isn't a lot of time in the morning, the rule is that the boys can't play until they're ready for school. Unaware that Todd had given him permission to do programming this morning, I chided Carter, which of course upset him. It's understandable, as he'd gotten mixed messages from us. I apologized to him and told him I didn't want to see him upset. I also suggested that he work on shutting off the computer without commotion when it's time, since he'll be able to go back on another time.

Presence. Do Your Best.

Wednesday, March 4 – No regrets!

I had another opportunity to practise empowered decision-making today.

I started out feeling particularly agitated this morning. Carter wanted to sing a song for me before I left for work, but Austin kept interrupting him. This caused Carter to have a bit of a tantrum. He *really* wanted to sing to me. I hadn't left any buffer time in my morning routine, so I needed to leave immediately to catch my train. When I told Carter that I was in a rush, it made matters worse. He got even more anxious and upset, and Austin freaked out too, wanting to perform the actions to Carter's song.

I had a choice to make: miss my train and listen to my boys sing a song that they had made up together and were so excited about, or catch my train and leave them in tears.

I chose to stay and listen.

Not only did Todd and I miss our regular train, but the following train was cancelled, so we're now almost forty minutes behind schedule, but there is no doubt that it was the right choice.

When things don't go according to my internal plan, I get frustrated. My inclination this morning was to displace my frustration by blaming Carter for it. Perhaps I can try to leave more buffer time in the morning to spend with the boys, though I usually spend a few minutes with them cuddling in bed before I get up. It's these moments that show how important these little people are in my life.

I know that if I hadn't stayed to listen to the song, I would have regretted it for the whole day. There's almost nothing worse than the feeling of regret. That's why I must pause in angry moments to have enough presence of mind to make the right choice. No regrets. The boys need to know that they're important, more than anything, and so are Todd and my family and friends. When there are so many demands on our time and schedules, we need to keep a clear perspective of what's really important.

And that's *people*. People are important. Our connections to each other are important. As Brené Brown poignantly describes in her widely acclaimed TED Talk, *The power of vulnerability*, "Connection is why we're here. It's what gives purpose and meaning to our lives."[35]

I'm on the train now, enjoying the quiet warmth, surrounded by people (two trainloads worth!) and the sun shining through the window. I have a different perspective.

The change in my emotions is remarkable, from hot anger when I first got into the car to my current serenity, having breathed and written through that anger to gain perspective. I missed my train. Seriously, what's the big deal anyway? Nothing is so important at work that couldn't wait. Besides, a slight change in routine is a good thing. Who knows? It may have exercised my brain a little and added creativity and productivity to my day.

Intention. Let Go. Purpose. Presence.

Monday, March 9 – Stuck—literally

It's dark again this morning, a big bright moon hanging in the sky. Daylight savings time began yesterday so we had to put our clocks back and lose an hour.

Friday afternoon brought me an interesting experience. We were on our way to meet with a board member of a bank that we regulate. On our way to the top floor of the old building she works in, the elevator suddenly jolted to a stop. It wasn't a large one, and there were seven of us in it. My mind leaped into action, imagining us stuck there for a long time and not being able to get out. My heart started racing and I began to feel light-headed. I felt the walls were closing in on me. I definitely have a bit of claustrophobia.

Breathe in. Breathe out.

I tried to keep my attention on my breath in the present moment. Fearful thoughts were forcing their way into my consciousness. My mind kept jumping ahead, picturing us slowly running out of air in the cramped space. Again and again, I gently turned back to my breath.

Breathe in. Breathe out.

The others in the elevator seemed relatively calm and relaxed. The building we were in housed a radio and television broadcasting company, so apart from my two colleagues and I, there were three producers and an executive assistant. We started chatting, mainly banter about being stuck in an elevator at first. That started to relax me. I added the conversation to my focus, staying quiet at first while I continued trying to steady my anxiety. Sounds of the conversation, my breath rising and falling, the sensations of my body.

While we waited for a technician to free us, we told stories to pass the time. My colleagues and I joked that the broadcasting folks would have to entertain us as we bank regulators wouldn't have nearly as interesting stories. By the end, I'd learned everyone's names: Reuben, Gabe, Mark, Christina. Reuben was eating a Reuben sandwich (no joke); Mark loves the opera. Apparently, Pavarotti had claustrophobia and sang in elevators to calm his nerves. Mark had spent the morning running from meeting to meeting, and this was the first break he'd had all day.

Sometimes a "crappy" situation can turn out to be positive. Those seventy-five minutes of being stuck were an unanticipated but perhaps much-needed break in all our respective routines, a chance to pause and connect with complete strangers. We even got a group selfie at the end. And I somehow succeeded, through mindful awareness, to overcome a fear that I've had almost my entire life. All I had to do was breathe! Amazing!

Presence. Let Go.

Thursday, March 12 – Training in action: Crucial Conversations

Today is my last day before vacation, and it's going to be a busy one. I wasn't feeling well last night with a headache, body aches, and low energy. I must be fighting a flu of some sort. I asked Todd to put the kids to bed so I could go to bed early. He joked that I'd have to be around for backup. When it was time to take the kids up to bed, he proceeded to lie down on Austin's bed and fall asleep!

Thank goodness for a training course I recently took at work, as I really needed those lessons in that moment. The course, called "Crucial Conversations," is about effective communication. The way we interact with each other can have dramatic impacts on our actions and relationships. Examples of communication issues include:

- Not speaking up and sharing important information when it's called for;
- Letting emotions take control, which can lead to misinformation, incomplete information, and assumptions;
- Making decisions based on assumptions and biases rather than facts;
- Not taking time to identify the emotions that may be behind others' words and actions;
- Failing to apologize or correct miscommunications, perhaps due to ego, pride, or the lack of ability to be vulnerable.

Strunk & White's *The Elements of Style* reminds us of the importance of effective communication: "Muddiness is not merely a disturber of prose, it is also a destroyer of life, of hope: death on the highway caused by a badly worded sign, heartbreak among lovers caused by a misplaced phrase in a well-intentioned letter . . ."[36]

Back to the situation at hand. While Todd was sleeping, I fought through my exhaustion to help the boys brush their teeth and get into bed, lying down with each of them to read stories. I then cleaned the kitchen, started the dishwasher, and took care of other miscellaneous tasks, such as writing Lolita a letter for her flight to the Philippines. Finally I was able to go to bed myself.

What a guy, that Todd! He apologized this morning, but by then I had cooled off. He was obviously tired and didn't do it on purpose. Some of the tools from my Crucial Conversations course helped me manage the situation. One is to separate facts from the story we tell ourselves and the assumptions we make about the situation. Another is to give others the benefit of the doubt before casting judgment, asking ourselves, "Why would a reasonable person behave this way?" Putting aside the story of "Todd is selfish and doesn't care that I'm not feeling well," I gave him the benefit of the doubt and thought about the facts: he had a very busy day; he tends to get tired out quickly, which may be partly due to his hypothyroidism. This reflection helped avert negative feelings, not to mention a possible fight. I think my mindful awareness practice also helped me to recognize my feelings and initial thoughts as well.

Thank you, mindfulness practice and Crucial Conversations!

Intention. Do Your Best.

Monday, March 30 – A different way of life

It's my first day back to work after our March break trip to Cuba.

Cuba was beautiful. Temperatures were great at around 30°C. It was such a wonderful trip; there's something about Cuba that

Todd and I just love. We took a day trip to Santiago de Cuba, a three-hour bus ride from the north end of the island in Holguin to the south by the Caribbean Sea. All the housing from one end of the island to the other was very similar in terms of size, style, etc. We saw televisions in some houses, but otherwise they seemed to contain just the necessities. As for transportation, there were people walking, riding bicycles, travelling by horse and carriage, and riding in the back of big pick-up trucks, packed tightly together. The very few cars we saw were quite old, from the 1950s. How resourceful the people must be to fix these old cars. I heard they use parts from other appliances, such as old dishwashers.

Observing Cuban society makes me think of the role consumer goods play in our own. Regardless of whether things still work or not, when they go out of style or start to look old, we simply replace them. I just donated a pair of shoes to Goodwill that were still in fairly good shape, but the heels were too chunky for today's style, so I never wore them. I also wonder if the kinds of consumer goods I own affect how I see myself (i.e., my ego). I likely judge myself based on what kind of clothes I wear, what car I drive, how big and fancy my house is . . . and so do others. Does owning these things make me happier or less happy?

The perspective I gain from seeing such a different way of life is priceless. On the one hand, I feel grateful for the everyday luxuries that I have. But what if these divert my attention from the simple pleasures in life, like spending time with family and in nature? What if my stuff has become a distraction from what really matters?

Cuba has a different political landscape than our democratic system, with a planned economy dominated by state-run enterprises. The Cuban government owns and operates most industries, and most of the labour force is employed by the state.

As our tour guide Eric said, every morning when Cubans wake up, they make a choice: they can be angry and miserable about what they don't have or they can choose to smile and play dominoes with friends and family. He chooses dominoes.

I think we have a choice too.

Presence. Gratitude.

Wednesday, April 8 – Work mode, parent mode

It's a rainy, cold morning. I'm missing the Cuban weather right about now.

Carter has had a few major blow-ups lately. Last night, he and Austin weren't listening when I repeatedly told them to get their jammies on and brush their teeth. They kept playing with toys in Carter's room. I counted to five and then proceeded to take the toys out of the room. While they were both mad, Carter started screaming uncontrollably, almost hyperventilating. This continued for at least fifteen minutes with no lessening of intensity. I sat with Carter trying to console him and understand his strong reaction. Austin was concerned and saw that Todd and I were as well. He came up to me with hugs and smiles, looking straight into my eyes, searching for comfort that everything would be okay. Finally I left the room to put Austin to bed while Todd stayed with Carter. He just sat with him without talking for a long time. Carter eventually calmed down and started reading a Minecraft book online.

Todd and I talked a lot about the incident. In retrospect, I wasn't being mindful. I was focusing on my agenda of getting the kids to bed; I was feeling like a bad parent, hurt because they weren't listening to me. My ego was activated. Carter and Austin need a parent who stays present with them. Maybe I could have played with them for a bit if I saw how engrossed they were in their play.

I need to transition more smoothly between work and home. I'd like to leave my results-oriented work hat at the door and enter into compassionate, patient parent mode when I come in. Funny—as I write this, I'm thinking I should always be compassionate and patient, not just as a parent. Maybe I'll be happier and less stressed at work if I drop the Type A personality traits. That's my goal, then: to stop taking myself and my work so seriously. I have a strong desire for approval and want to do a really good job, so I aim high. This is probably not all bad, but I can probably do even better if I keep it in perspective.

It's a slow train ride this morning. I'll take this as an additional sign to slow down and enjoy the journey. There is a quiet hum of conversation around me.

Presence. Intention. Let Go. Balance. Do Your Best.

Thursday, April 9 – A good day!

Despite the rainy, miserable weather, yesterday was great. At work, I was calm, productive, and engaged with my staff. When I got home, I was ready to be present with Carter, who was in good spirits. We went to math night at his school, which was very nice. There were activities, games, and information on the math curriculum. Math is being taught differently than when I was a kid. Now, it's much more about thinking and talking through number problems than memorizing. This seems like a practical approach, with plenty of transferable skills that the kids will be able to apply throughout their life. I'm sure I've forgotten half the stuff I memorized as a child. My favourite part about the night was stepping into Carter's world, the part I don't usually get to witness. He saw many of his friends, and I chatted with other parents I've met through various school and community events.

Alas, today is another cold, dark, rainy day, so we'll see what lies ahead. I have my commuting buddy back after Todd was away at a doctor's appointment yesterday. I'm so grateful for my family. I love them so much.

Presence. Balance. Gratitude.

Tuesday, April 14 – Gratitude and empathy

Last night, I went to a wonderful talk hosted at the boys' school. The guest speaker, Dr. Karyn Gordon, spoke about teaching our children empathy and gratitude. As I am learning through Dr. Shefali's lessons on parenting, I have to understand myself first before trying to help my children. I suppose it's hard to be an effective role model if I'm not practising what I preach. It's kind of like the safety procedures on an airplane: parents are supposed to put on their own oxygen mask before putting on a child's. I have to **take care of myself first so I'm able to help others.** This is such an important concept. How can I properly care for others if my own needs are not met and I'm not happy?

My takeaway as a leader, mother, and daughter is to ensure I maintain a responsibility *to* people, not *for* them. By feeling responsible *for* people, I risk burnout. It also discourages personal accountability in those who are under my wing. I can definitely think of times where I've wanted to help others and felt responsible for their decisions, actions, and inaction. If they didn't follow my advice, I felt as if I'd failed them. It's likely that I inadvertently push too hard for them to do what I think is best. A particularly salient example is when I tried so hard to help my mom overcome her stockpiling tendencies. I read books on the topic and gave her strategies. I even hired her a professional organizer. But I learned the hard way that people need to want to change and be ready to do the work. I can't force my vision on them through my own sheer will. My meddling caused a strain on our relationship for a while.

Understanding that **we are not responsible for others** and **we can't control others' behaviour** has been very liberating. I can now accept that my mom prefers to work on her issue by herself. I simply let her know that I'm here whenever she needs me. It's a much healthier relationship.

Dr. Gordon also discussed different "characters": Grateful George, Entitled Elliott, and Negative Nelly. Entitled Elliott and Negative Nelly represent typical default behaviours: Entitled Elliott takes things for granted and has high expectations of himself and others. Negative Nelly has a glass-half-empty perspective on life; she's quick to point out problems rather than solutions. Grateful George is the character who doesn't feel owed the many positive things in life and is grateful for them. He sees life from a glass-half-full perspective. Personally, I need to work on becoming more like Grateful George and less like Entitled Elliott.

According to Dr. Gordon, practising gratitude literally changes our brain. She suggests that everyone keep a gratitude journal. I guess I'm on the right track! I'll focus even more on gratitude in my journal from now on.

Here are six things I'm grateful for today:
- The hugs and kisses from the boys this morning.
- The sunshine.

- My awesome commuting buddy, Todd.
- My mom and my relationship with her. Her love and dedication to parenting provided my siblings and I with the best upbringing I could ask for.
- Lolita. All she does with the boys and her help around the house.
- My engaging and challenging job, where I get to learn on a daily basis and work with people.

Gratitude. Let Go.

Wednesday, April 15 – Foundations

Today, I'm thankful for the morning with my boys, the sunshine and blue sky, a job that offers some flexibility, my health, and the health of my family. I'm also thankful for my mom and dad, who gave me such a solid foundation in my childhood. I think about this often—how important my parents are in my life, the values they instilled in me, the opportunities they've provided.

Growing up, my family was not wealthy—not in terms of monetary wealth, anyway. We rarely ate out for dinner, and we never went to Disney World or traveled outside the country. But my mother found opportunities for her kids to have meaningful travel experiences regardless. When my sister Heather and I were teenagers, she enrolled us in an exchange trip. We stayed with families in Saskatchewan, and in return, teens from Saskatchewan stayed with us. Heather and I were paired with two cousins from Craik, a small town outside Moose Jaw. As a result, we took our first airplane trip, experienced living in a different province, and met wonderful people. (Hi, Trudy! Hi, Tammy!)

My mom is well-educated and follows the news closely. She's been ahead of her time on various social issues like climate change. To make a point, one day, she had us show up at McDonald's with our own plates and cutlery. It was her way of protesting all the waste created by Styrofoam takeout containers. It was embarrassing as a child because taking part in her protests made me stand out. But looking back, I truly appreciate where she was coming from, and her lessons have stuck with me. It's more important to act according to our values and make a difference than blend in with the crowd.

Even now, I get some questioning looks when people see me writing in a journal. It must look pretty old school to them. There's something about going off the beaten path that I like. I try not to be self-conscious. Different can be good.

Love. Gratitude. Purpose.

Friday, April 17 – Quiet presence and purpose

Today would have been my paternal grandma's 103rd birthday. I remember her with loving memories. My siblings and I were fortunate to have grown up with her, living in the same farmhouse that my dad grew up in. She had her own bedroom and sitting room, but otherwise we shared the house. She loved to travel and watch soap operas. My siblings and I weren't allowed to watch soap operas, but we'd sneak into her room and join her in front of the TV, and she wouldn't tell on us. Her sitting room was full of little keepsakes she'd picked up during her various trips around the globe. The walls were adorned with dolls, statues, decorative plates, and pictures. She was a quiet and respectful person, cautious in her approach with the family, preferring not to interfere with my parents' decisions. She was a big woman and I just loved sitting on her knee to cuddle, nestled against her warm body.

When I was a teenager, she suffered a stroke and moved into a long-term care facility. She lived there for a few years before she passed away.

Her quiet, passive presence, and later, her lessened capacity for enjoyment due to physical and mental limitations, didn't mean her life was devoid of purpose. I'm reminded of Viktor E. Frankl's views on the purpose of life in *Man's Search For Meaning*: "An active life serves the purpose of giving man the opportunity to realize values in creative work, while a passive life of enjoyment affords him the opportunity to obtain fulfillment in experiencing beauty, art, or nature. But there is also purpose in that life which is almost barren of both creation and enjoyment and which admits of but one possibility of high moral behaviour: namely, in man's attitude to his existence, an existence restricted by external forces."[37] Frankl, a neurologist and psychiatrist, wrote his book after he experienced living in a Nazi concentration camp during World War II. I find his perspective helpful and comforting: life itself has a purpose, and it isn't about what we achieve or accomplish—just *being* has meaning. Throughout our lives, we move through different stages of meaning and purpose. As babies, we start out living passively, then become active as adults. As we age and face physical barriers, we naturally cycle back to passive lives.

It's a liberating perspective.

Purpose. Balance. Let Go. Gratitude.

Monday, April 20 – Boundaries

It's a rainy, cool Monday morning. Our weekend was filled with lots of nice family time and some challenges too.

On Saturday, the four of us went out of town to my nephew's birthday. We then headed straight to Carter's breakdance class, and finally out to dinner at Swiss Chalet. When we got home, Carter and Austin proceeded to get their bikes out. It was a beautiful evening, just before eight o'clock. Although it was very close to the boys' bedtime, I figured a quick ride back and forth on the sidewalk wouldn't do any harm. Boy, was I wrong! When it was time for them to come inside, they were completely disobedient and crossed the street instead.

I was livid. I felt completely out of control. So mad!

My initial reaction was to ban bike use, yell and scream. But I managed to sit with the strong emotions and say some calm words to Carter before going upstairs to put Austin to bed. Carter fell asleep on the couch downstairs, still not listening.

That night, Todd and I had a strategic parenting session. We brought out some of our parenting books, including *The Conscious Parent* by Dr. Shefali and *How To Talk So Your Kids Will Listen & Listen So Your Kids Will Talk* by Adele Faber and Elaine Mazlich. We came up with a more defined bedtime schedule: 7:30 pm is upstairs and 8:00 pm is lights out. If the kids are too slow to get upstairs and ready for bed, then they miss out on a bedtime story. I think we've been too flexible, so now they're pushing boundaries to the point of being ineffective. We have to make it a priority to stick to the boundaries we set. In retrospect, because of the long, busy day we had, allowing them to get on their bikes at that hour was not a good idea, especially without setting clear expectations of how much time they'd have on them.

I'm sure I've fallen into the working mom trap—since I haven't seen them as much as I'd like during the day, bedtime stretches out so I can squeeze in some extra time with them at the end of the day.

The next day, on the drive over to a family dinner to celebrate my mother- and father-in-law's 50th wedding anniversary, we had a great conversation. We talked about family values and the importance of being a team, listening to each other and working together. We also showed them the new bedtime schedule, which we'd printed out. It was clear and simple. That evening, bedtime went pretty well. Carter wasn't going to make it too easy, but we stuck to it and told him that he would have less story time as a consequence of not getting to bed on time.

Intention. Presence. Balance.

Tuesday, April 21 – Testing and gratitude

I had a nice evening last night volunteering at Carter's Beaver Scouts. I'm working toward becoming a Scout leader, with five hours of online training left to complete. It's a lengthy process! Carter was pretty happy to have me there with him. He's still picking battles with Todd and me, but I'm quick to recognize it now. As we were leaving Beavers, Carter asked if he could go on YouTube when he got home. Based on the way he asked, I got the feeling that he knew the answer and was testing me. Rather than saying no, I put the question back to him. What did he think, based on the time of night and what he knew about his bedtime schedule? He kept pressing me, demanding an answer. I had to practise patience and ruthless compassion all night as he continued to ask these types of questions, threatening to explode at any trigger on my part. It turned out okay.

As we go through these challenges, I'm thankful for my crew . . .

Todd, a great partner in challenging moments with Carter. We work as a team, so one can take the lead when the other is starting to lose patience.

Carter, the sweet, sensitive, empathetic boy that he is. He has a good sense of humour and I love sharing a laugh with him. He comes up with pretty good jokes.

Austin, with his bright, cheery, upfront demeanour. You always know where you stand with Austin. He has a smart silliness that makes you smile and brightens your day.

I'm also grateful for the day itself, the sun brightening the earth around us. And of course, for my coffee. *Mmm*, coffee.

Presence. Gratitude. Intention.

Friday, April 24 – My biggest teacher

I worked from home on Wednesday and took Austin to his doctor's appointment. In the doctor's office, I noticed posters on the wall about anxiety in children, so I asked her about it. We talked about Carter, who continues to have episodes every day now. In the last one, he wanted to continue playing football in the basement after bedtime. He was yelling, crying, and repeating, "I need to play football, I need to play football!" He covered his ears when I tried to talk to him. This continued on and off until he finally fell asleep from exhaustion.

I mentioned to the doctor that he's obsessed with the computer game Minecraft. She said that Minecraft has addictive qualities because it provides instant gratification. She has seen it cause similar behavioural issues in many children. She asked whether all his caregivers have consistent expectations and suggested that Carter may be experiencing confusion from differences. We talked about whether he could be acting out to get attention. She advised me to ignore or walk away from the behaviour after calmly stating why it's not possible for him to do what he wants. Pointing to a written schedule is a good idea as it keeps engaging in the behaviour to a minimum. I will focus on giving him positive attention during more tranquil times.

I talked to Carter that night, pointing out my observations about the trends in his behaviour. I mentioned that there's a session he could go to with other kids to help him find ways to cope with his strong emotions. He seemed receptive. He's a very sweet boy, just full of emotions that I don't think he understands.

The following night was a bit better. We still can't entirely avoid the episodes when it comes to transition times. I bring the schedule over to Carter and point to it to remind him of our regular routine. Essentially, he comes home from school, has a snack, does some homework, then gets on the computer. Rather than actually playing Minecraft, he watches YouTube videos of other people playing. He's on the computer for about an hour and a half and just wants more, more, more. It's never enough time. Our new plan is no computer during the week until he can earn it with behaviours that fall in line with our family values: listening, showing respect for each other, no yelling at each other, and taking care of ourselves, our house, our belongings, and the environment. We have the list stuck on our fridge. We'll see how this plan goes.

Insecure questions arise about our parenting. Are Todd and I away too much? Do the boys need us to be around more? We try hard to focus on spending quality time together when we're home, but is it enough? Maybe one of us should take a break from the workforce so there is always a parent at home with them. Parenting these two kids is the most important job we have.

Todd found an article on addiction in kids that suggested it could be related to lack of parental involvement and connection, particularly the mother. *Gasp!* Guilt is washing over me as I sit here. What to do? What a painful way to start my day, worrying about my son. Todd and I will continue reading and strategizing together. It's not easy, but we'll work through it. We love Carter so much.

Now, for the gratitude part of my journal entry . . . I must say, as I reflect on the challenges we're having with Carter right now, I'm thankful for him and what he's teaching me about myself. He's my reminder to *slow down* and listen. I get so caught up in *doing* and trying to please others that I forget to just *be*. I put a lot of expectations on myself about what I should be doing. But I could also think of myself as being perfect the way I am, right now. Perfectly imperfect, as I like to say. Things I do will not change that. Carter is my reminder. He is my teacher in this way.

Presence. Gratitude. Intention. Do Your Best.

Friday, May 1 – Unclogging the flute

It's hard to believe that it's May already. Perhaps this thought means that I need to slow down, as time is flying by. It's a slightly cool, cloudy morning.

I love how life ebbs and flows—I can never entirely predict where it will take me. That's how I feel about my job. I'm enjoying it now, but I always want to be open to change if needed.

I'm really thankful for being a mom. For quite a while, Todd and I didn't know if we would have the opportunity to be parents. Two years of doctor's appointments, fertility treatments, and a nagging feeling that the life we had envisaged was slipping away from us. In the end, it was a big lesson about the connection between mind and body.

My good friend Janis, who worked at a hospital in downtown Toronto, introduced me to her friend that worked in the fertility clinic. We had a candid discussion about my diagnosis, unexplained infertility, and the treatments I was undergoing. After we'd gone over everything in detail, she paused, looked me straight in the eye, and said, "There is nothing wrong with you." She recommended a book called *Taking Charge of Your Fertility* and told me that if I followed the book's instructions, I would become pregnant. Her reassurance was exactly what I needed to shift my mindset from "What's wrong with me?" to "I got this." It was my very next cycle when Carter was conceived.

My own mind had become an obstacle to conceiving a child. With each failed cycle, it was consumed afresh by the fear that I would never get pregnant. Negative thoughts were blocking my body from doing its thing.

I now realize that I can take responsibility for my mind and let doubtful thoughts pass through me. My mind and body connect harmoniously if I quiet anxious thoughts and let the energy flow. I have to stop holding myself back.

At a session with Eckhart's partner Kim Eng, a spiritual teacher herself, she analogized humans to flutes: life's energy wants to flow through us, but the mind can clog the flute. All we need to do is unclog our flutes to allow the energy to flow, unlocking our true potential. [38]

Today, I am particularly thankful for the kindness of strangers—strangers who may never know the impact they've had on someone's life simply by taking the time to share words of support. I only hope that I can pay it forward in some small way.

May we all take the time to unclog our flutes.

Presence. Gratitude. Let Go.

Monday, May 11 – Roller Coaster

It's a foggy, cool Monday morning. I'm taking a slightly later train, having eked out a few extra minutes with the boys rather than rush out the door.

It's been a roller coaster of emotions the last few days.

Thursday night, I went to a Mental Health Awareness session at a local public school. One of the speakers was a psychologist who had a very informative presentation. In the Q & A, I asked about Carter and his recent behaviour with his computer game. She confirmed that he is experiencing addict behaviour and advised that we get help. Essentially, she said, the object of the addiction—in Carter's case, the computer game—becomes a perceived *need* for the child, who uses whatever means they can to obtain it. It makes sense, but it still kind of scared me to hear it.

Friday was a great day for Carter. We distracted him in healthy ways, playing football in the backyard. At one point he said, "Mommy, I haven't gone on my computer yet," and I replied, "If you want to go on the computer today, you better go now because it's only twenty minutes until bedtime." He chose to stay outside with us. I felt really happy about that.

Unfortunately, Saturday was not a good day. He went on the computer for fifteen minutes in the morning and then had a tough time turning it off. We were pushing him because he had to get to his flag football game, and it was our turn to bring snacks. It all went downhill from there. He refused to get out of the car when we got to the field, so he didn't participate in the game at all. He was obsessed with his computer for the rest of the day, asking for permission to play, then freaking out when the answer wasn't what he wanted to hear. I was emotional and didn't handle the situation well at all. His constant pleas, "I need to go on the computer. Can I go on the computer? I need to go on the computer . . ." were grating on me. It was a difficult day for me and I don't think I made it any easier on him.

Todd took him to his breakdance class in the afternoon. I had offered to drive at first, but Carter politely asked if Daddy could take him instead. And then, realizing that it might hurt my feelings, he came up to me and asked so sweetly if it was okay and if I didn't mind. He is such a thoughtful boy; it melted my heart. I told him I didn't mind, but immediately after they left, I went upstairs and had a good cry.

It was a beautiful day, so I walked over to the birthday party Austin was at to pick him up. The walk did wonders for my mood. I took in the sunshine and the green leaves around me. Then, my friend

Nicole and I arranged to walk around the trails in our neighbourhood together. Our chat on the beautiful trail made me feel even lighter. I needed these mindful moments. I had gotten lost in my thoughts and emotions.

I am forever grateful and thankful for my amazing support network. Over the last couple of weeks, Todd, my mom, Jai, Heather, Janis, Emily, and Nicole have been truly amazing in helping me get through these challenges. I am so lucky! I'm so grateful for Carter and Austin, too, for continuing to teach me so much, along with brightening my days. I'm thankful for the education system and the tools and resources it offers parents and children. I'm thankful for my health and my family's health. Truly thankful.

Gratitude. Balance. Presence. Do Your Best.

Wednesday, May 13 – Asking for help

It's a cool, cloudy morning, around 7°C. *Brrr.* Back to coats.

We had a great day yesterday. Todd, Carter, Austin, and I all went to see a counsellor at a walk-in clinic. Carter was in a good mood. He got his work done in class, did his homework, and didn't go on the computer for two days. The counsellor had him fill out a form to express how happy he was on a scale of one to ten, one being the least happy and ten being the happiest. Carter gave himself a four after using the computer, and an eight when he didn't go on the computer for the day. We talked about things that Todd and I can do to help him manage his really big feelings, and things that Carter can do himself. The counsellor gave us two lists, one for Todd and I and one for Carter. Our list was very long while Carter's was quite short.

This was the "Mom and Dad" list:

- Give Carter warnings as it gets close to screen time being over.
- Label Carter's feelings: sad, frustrated, etc.
- Be there for Carter and stay calm. Tell him we get it, we understand how he's feeling.
- Watch for warning signs, physical or behavioural.
- Give Carter choices during transition time. For example, rather than simply tell him to get off the computer, ask, "What would you like to do now, have a snack or go outside to play?"

This was Carter's list:

- Take deep breaths.
- Remind himself, "It's okay, I'll get to go on the computer later."

It's amazing just how much parents' behaviour influences children. It was mostly Todd and I who needed help from the counsellor, not Carter. He's just acting and reacting as any kid would. It's up to us, as his parents, to set appropriate boundaries and communicate expectations clearly. It was another "Aha" moment.

Carter woke up feeling very happy and loving this morning. Austin was still sleeping when we left.

We'll take it one day at a time.

I'm thankful for counsellors, who are so caring and compassionate and share their gifts with those who need tools. I'm thankful for my supportive spouse. I'm thankful for all the quiet, early morning commuters we share a ride with every morning.

Gratitude. Balance. Do Your Best.

Thursday, May 14 – Strategies in action

Brrr, it's another chilly morning for May, but sunny with a clear blue sky.

We had a nice evening yesterday. The boys played in the basement while Todd and I did our seven-minute workout. Carter had asked in the morning and then again after school if he could play on the computer, so we gave him and Austin twenty minutes. Carter got tense during his computer time, especially toward the end, so he used the deep breathing strategy the counsellor had given him. Todd and I also used our strategies: naming his emotions, giving him warnings before it was time to finish. Carter did really well. I was so proud of him.

At night, we read *Moody Cow Meditates* by Kerry Lee MacLean as a bedtime story. It's a really great book that Nicole lent me about how to handle all those bad-day types of feelings (spoiler: put them in a jar in the form of sparkles and let them slowly sink to the bottom of the jar).

I have so many ideas for activities I'd love to do with the boys—I just wish I had more time to do them. The perpetual issue is finding the right balance. Sometimes it doesn't seem too bad, especially if I'm able to take advantage of my evenings with them. I actually rated myself as a nine out of ten on the happiness scale the counsellor gave us yesterday. I am grateful for so much in my life right now.

Gratitude. Balance.

Friday, May 22 – Things we take for granted

On Sunday, we met up with Jai and Steve, their daughter Delainey, and Stu at my mom and dad's. Mom is away on a cruise with my aunt, so my dad is home alone. It was a beautiful day, so we sat outside, tried to fly a kite, and played football, volleyball, and soccer.

It was really nice hanging out at my parents' property. It's one of the amazing things from my childhood I can easily take for granted. The property is eleven acres, with a large open field out front. Along the driveway is a hand-built stone wall that the kids love playing on, and tall trees that are perfect for climbing. The old barn is still standing, with long ropes my dad fixed to the rafters to swing from, and a big pile of hay to jump into from the barn's upper floor.

In the long, hazy months of summer, my siblings and I would wade through the creek that runs behind the house, build rafts, and catch tadpoles. In the winter, when the creek overflowed and froze, we'd put on our ice skates and slide around the bumpy surface, the quiet beauty of nature surrounding us.

These memories are of simpler times, when the world seemed to move at a slower pace. Though I complained to my mother of being bored in the summer and wished I could play with other children, I'm sure that the large natural spaces and uninterrupted time to explore were more impactful than I appreciated at the time.

I'm feeling very fortunate and grateful for family, my foundations, and the beautiful land that surrounds us.

Gratitude. Presence.

Friday, May 29 – The show

This morning on the GO train, I am closer to the earth than I was during my Monday morning commute to Ottawa by plane. From the small oval window of the plane, the land below looked so elegantly cut out. The buildings stood in neat little clusters throughout the city, and the partially frozen water of Lake Ontario created a beautiful pattern around its edges. There is so much beauty in the world around us. I just need to slow down and pause long enough to enjoy it. My morning commute is a perfect opportunity.

I look out the GO train window, past the reflections that are mirrored there. It's like straining to see beyond the "show" of my life, my perception of reality, to glimpse the essence of the world around me. Like pulling away the stories my mind tells about my past and future to uncover the pure, raw reality of the present moment without judgment. I remind myself that it is always there, in all its stillness, peace, and perfection. But my mind creates a layer of fog that obscures the peace. All I have to do is disperse the fog. My thought patterns are so deeply ingrained, it is much easier said than done.

My "show" is not so bad, though, and I am very grateful for it; I just have to keep in mind that it is but a story in a much larger picture. The stresses at work and the challenges at home are all just part of the show.

Presence. Gratitude. Balance.

Thursday, June 11 – Can't say "no!"

It was an interesting day yesterday. It all started with Carter's school's spring carnival, an end-of-year party that a group of parent volunteers organize every year. It is quite elaborate with bouncy castles, sumo wrestling, ice cream trucks, BBQ, watermelon eating contests . . . The list goes on.

This year, a friend of mine was planning a cake walk and asked if I could bake a cake to contribute. I agreed even though baking is not a talent or an interest of mine. My practical side sees it as an unproductive use of time as it involves making something full of sugar, which is not healthy, and we don't need more unhealthy food in our lives. I know, I'm a total buzzkill. I justified it to myself as a fun activity to do with the boys on the weekend, which it was. Really, though, I am just not good at saying "no." After running out of supplies and having to bike to the grocery store midway through the process, I ended up making two cakes. One of these, the four of us ate as part of a little end-of-year celebration for all the work we did at our respective schools and workplaces. It was nice.

As for the spring carnival cake . . . It was a very hot and windy day. With little baking experience, I didn't think to put the cake in the refrigerator. And I didn't have a proper cake box either. I was doomed. There I was, walking to the front doors of the school with a plate holding my cake covered in plastic wrap, the heat melting the icing and the wind blowing the plastic off. What a disaster! I couldn't possibly show up with that sad-looking cake. I ran back to the car, too embarrassed to let anyone see my major cake fail, and brought it back home.

Wait, that sounds like my ego, worrying about how I would be perceived!

Todd, Carter, and I had a good laugh about the whole thing. I felt bad for letting down my friend, but I think she persuaded enough people to bring cakes that there were plenty, despite my omission.

It may have been a wasted effort, but it was also a reminder not to take things too seriously. I suppose these are the kinds of events that result in memorable life lessons.

I recognize that I have to practise saying "no" more often so I can be intentional with my time.

Intention. Balance. Let Go.

Friday, June 19 – Disappointments are opportunities to grow

It has not been a picture-perfect morning. Carter is having a tantrum because it's pyjama day at school and he's allowed to bring a stuffy. The problem? He *loves* wolves right now and really wants to bring a stuffed wolf, but he doesn't have one. Todd and I both looked for one yesterday but didn't have any luck. Carter's having a hard time dealing with it this morning. I suggested to Todd that, in fact, this disappointment may be good for him. It might help him learn how to deal with future disappointments in his life. We can't always protect him from things not going his way. I have to remember that he's only seven years old and this behaviour is not unusual.

Carter's plight reminds me of one of my own. It was the 1980s, and I was a young girl in grade 3. Cabbage Patch Kids (CPK) were all the rage and I wanted one so badly—those pudgy limbs, the baby powder scent, those big eyes and awesome hairstyles. They even came with their own birth certificate. Having a unique CPK of my own was my dream. Alas, at that time, the doll was just too expensive for my family. They sold for around forty dollars each, and if I got one, my two sisters would have to get one too (my mom being dedicated to fairness). One hundred and twenty dollars was outside of my family's budget for toys. Meanwhile, all my classmates had one, including my best friend, Jill. Jill kept telling me that Cecilia, her CPK, needed a best friend. So I started to save up, determined to pay for the doll myself. Unfortunately, for an eight-year-old, it was a slow process. I really didn't have much money coming in, my allowance being in cents, not dollars.

After many months, I wasn't much closer to my goal, and my grandma felt bad for me. Under her budget constraints, she did what she could, and one day a Pumpkin Patch Kid (PPK) showed up on our doorstep. I had mixed emotions: appreciation, but also embarrassment. A PPK was nowhere near as cool as a CPK. None of my friends had even heard of a PPK. It was essentially a knock-off, and it didn't have the same scent or come with its own birth papers. On the bright side, Tiffany (I got to name her myself—I guess that was a benefit) was still a best friend for Cecilia. So, in the end, I made the best of it. Eventually, I saved up enough money for a proper CPK as well: Carla Kate. She was perfect, with a blonde side ponytail, big green eyes, and a cool jean jacket. Tiffany and Carla Kate became good friends. It may have been after the CPK fad had subsided and I no longer played with dolls quite so much, but it was a goal that I persevered toward and finally met. It was satisfying.

The lessons my quest taught me have served me well over the years: hard work, patience, acceptance, and appreciation. Had I been given that CPK when I first wanted it, I would have missed out on all those lessons.

This morning I am grateful for Carter and the struggles we share, Austin's bright, happy self, Todd, who is such a supportive partner, our home, my job, my colleagues, and the quiet commuters that surround me on the train.

Balance. Gratitude.

Wednesday, June 24 – Passions make the world go round

I got Carter and Austin stuffies as end-of-school-year gifts. I finally found a stuffed wolf for Carter, well, something close: a stuffed husky. It was his equivalent of the Pumpkin Patch Kid. He was kind of hesitant about it at first, then later quietly said to me, "I really like the husky, Mom, thank you." It was such a small gesture of gratitude, but it made my heart so happy.

Carter's obsession with wolves runs deep. Wolves are the subject of his poems, research projects, and presentations. He talks about them all the time.

Austin's current passion is soccer. Austin wakes up and puts on a soccer jersey every morning to wear to school. He had a blast playing soccer with kids three years older than him at a Beaveree camp last weekend, and easily kept up with them. He's so small but very quick, and he seems to have natural instincts for the game, especially on defence. It was so enjoyable watching him play into the evening.

Todd continues to be fascinated with computers. Sharing a passion, he and Carter work on programming projects together, including setting up servers so Carter and his friends can play Minecraft as a group.

If I was to name a passion of mine, it would have to be people. I love people. I enjoy getting to know them, helping them, cheering them on, and being with them. It's great to honour each other's passions and watch the boys explore interests that resonate with them and make them happy.

Todd and I were musing about the athletes competing in the Pan Am Games, which are happening in Toronto this year. What motivates them to work so hard for a few competitions like the Olympics, which only come once every four years? We heard a radio program where they were talking about the limited interest in women's sports, leaving female athletes without the option of a full-time job in their field. Their motivation must come from within and relate to a personal passion and purpose.

We all have our own drives. We may not understand each others' passions, goals, and desires, but the fact that we are all different is what makes the world so wonderfully diverse. We need diversity and balance for the economy. Imagine if we were all interested in the same things and all vied for the same type of work. We need each other to bring different skill sets and interests to the table and work together to (hopefully) better the world and meet the various needs of our citizens. It really is a beautiful thing to think about our interconnectivity. While a little competition can be a good thing, we also need each other just the way we are, and the more we appreciate how we fit together to make the world a better place, the happier we will be.

Purpose. Balance.

Monday, July 6 – Finding love

Yesterday, Todd and I celebrated our twelfth wedding anniversary. I am so grateful for being married to such a wonderful man. I love his intellect and his humour, and I enjoy spending time with him, even quiet commuting time where he's reading the news and I'm writing in my journal. You know you're comfortable with someone when sitting in silence with them is a slice of divine peace.

I feel very lucky that I met Todd and found such a compatible life partner in him. Love is a funny thing. Not to sound cliché, but I would call him my soul mate. I don't believe that there's only one soul mate out there for everyone; that's just not practical. But I do believe there is something special that deeply attracts two people beyond physical attraction.

In my university days, I had a debate with some of my philosophy classmates. There were four of us, studying late into the night before a test the next day. At around two o'clock in the morning, we got into a heated discussion about what makes someone fall in love with someone else. Two of us believed in what we might describe as soul mates while the others argued that falling in love can be explained through science. For example, some studies in psychology conclude that we tend to be attracted to people who look like us. In my own experience, while I've been physically attracted to plenty of people, there have been very few with whom I've felt both a physical and an emotional connection. I don't think science can fully explain falling in love. Why one person and not another? I think there's a deeper explanation, something at the level of the soul. That's why I feel especially lucky that my path crossed with Todd's in high school.

Even though we dated in high school, as I've mentioned, we weren't together for over seven years after that. During that period, I started to feel left behind when it came to love. Sure, I dated, but I didn't have any serious relationships. After university, I was surrounded by people who all seemed to have found love. My sisters were both in long-term relationships (to their now husbands), and so were my roommates and best friends. To make matters worse, a guy I had recently dated said to me, "What's wrong with you, why are you the only one without a serious boyfriend?" I wanted to shoot back (and maybe did), "*You* tell *me*, what's wrong with me?" In retrospect, I'm sure he was just reflecting back the energy I was emitting. Indeed, I felt like there was something wrong with me. I started doubting my worth until I read *In The Meantime: Finding Yourself And The Love You Want* by Iyanla Vanzant. That's when I learned **the valuable lesson of loving myself.** After reading the book, my mindset shifted from focusing on what I didn't have (i.e., a boyfriend) to focusing on what I did have, and on loving myself. I stopped feeling sorry for myself because I was the only one not in a long-term relationship. I started enjoying my time alone. I worked out regularly, revelling in the time I had to take care of my body. I read books and did things I enjoyed. I went out to clubs with my friends and danced the night away.

It wasn't long after this mindset shift that it felt like the universe shifted with me. Now, when I went on a date, I was in the moment, not worrying about what the future held for the burgeoning relationship. I was happy with myself and satisfied with enjoying whatever time I spent with others. If a date didn't turn into a long-term relationship, that was okay. And then, along came Todd back into my life. He had broken up with his university girlfriend and was back in town for the Christmas holidays. We met up at a restaurant in Toronto to catch up. I felt the spark. And the rest, as they say, is history.

Love. Presence.

Friday, July 10 – Everybody's working for the weekend

The sun is shining high this morning, so I'm trying to take it in and enjoy the moment. I know when I get to the office it'll be nonstop like it has been for the rest of the week. It's been a long five days.

After my maternity leave with Carter, I went back to work for just three days a week. While this may have seemed like a career-limiting decision, it turned out quite the opposite. I ended up going from an individual bank supervision team to leading an enterprise-wide project, which led to my involvement in an international working group. In this role, I worked closely with members of our executive team. It was a wonderful balance, as I could fully enjoy my time with my one-year-old baby boy while looking forward to my time at the office. When I was there, I was fully engaged and energized to be using my brain in an intellectually stimulating way. As the project intensified, I increased my work schedule to four days a week, and it still felt like a decent balance. They were four long days with no coffee breaks, but it was rewarding to feel so productive and spend the fifth day of the week with baby Carter, getting household errands done.

Honestly, the four-day workweek felt like a sustainable sweet spot. Five days of focusing on work, including a long commute, make it too easy for me to get caught up in my work life at the expense of other things I value. It's too easy to lose my balance and let work projects take on a disproportionate level of importance. Plus, the remaining two days end up being dedicated to preparing for the five working days. They're consumed with activities such as grocery shopping, meal preparation, house cleaning, and laundry. There is such limited time left to actually live and take care of family, friends, and community. This is how unmindful behaviour creeps in. I get sucked into the routine, losing my creativity and my perspective of the big picture.

I've read about other countries, mainly in Europe, where shorter workweeks have become the norm with positive results, including increased productivity. Germany is an example: they have fewer working hours a year than their British counterparts, and yet, stats have shown them to be almost thirty percent more productive.[39]

In the meantime, vacation and leave options suit me, so I'll try to use these to achieve the balance that is so important in life. I really enjoy my job and have been getting a lot of satisfaction from it, but boy, do I ever love spending time with my boys. Having conversations with them and sharing experiences is so fulfilling. I don't want to end up "working for the weekend."

When I shared my views about the benefits of the four-day workweek at a family get-together, I got a lot of nodding heads, with the exception of my dad. My dad wondered whatever happened to the sixth working day of the week. He's a mechanic and runs his own business, working Monday to Saturday. He's seventy-two years old and doesn't show much desire to retire. It may be a generational thing. And perhaps it makes a difference what the job is, as I believe he really enjoys what he does as well. It's like a hobby for him.

It really is all about balance, passion, and intention. I have to find what works for me personally and make conscious choices about my lifestyle, aligned with my own purpose and passions. What I don't want to do is sacrifice the current day for a future day. I want to enjoy every day of my life.

The fact that this conversation triggered me may be an indication that I need to improve my current balance. I will meditate on that this morning while I enjoy my coffee.

Intention. Gratitude. Balance.

Tuesday, July 14 – Autopilot (and my birthday!)

It's a warm but cloudy morning, with thunderstorms expected later.

It's also my birthday! Thirty-nine years young. The older I get, the faster time seems to go. Is it because of the habits and routines I get caught up in? Or maybe it's a relative thing, as the denominator—the number of years I've been alive—keeps increasing, so proportionately, each increment of time (say, a year) keeps shrinking in relation to my age.

I've heard psychologists and neurologists attribute this phenomenon to how we experience our lives. As children, everything is new to us, so we're constantly building memories, attuned to all the details and experiencing everything fully. As we get older, our brains build efficiencies to save energy and take the path of least resistance—in other words, autopilot. Routine tasks get built into neural pathways that become automatic.[40]

Unfortunately, while autopilot helps with efficiency, there's a risk of failing to build new pathways. When we aren't fully present and noticing what's happening around us, we're less likely to be building new memories. Therefore, time feels like it's moving faster.[41] Another downside to autopilot is our brain doesn't get adequate exercise leading to issues like forgetfulness.

To help combat this, neurologists recommend doing things that break up your regular routine, like taking a different route to work every day. I tried a simple test to gain awareness of my default setting: I took off my watch and put it on the opposite wrist. As I continued to look at the wrong wrist throughout the day, even hours after I'd moved my watch, I saw clear evidence of my brain on autopilot. I've also experienced it when driving: I sometimes arrive at my destination and barely remember how I got there. I was likely lost in thought and operating on autopilot.

Same goes for my day-to-day commuting routine. One day I became alive to it: as I walked by Union Station that morning, there was a man offering to tell a joke for a quarter. I glanced up from my phone, smiled politely, and said, "No thanks." An automatic response.

Why no joke? Wouldn't it have been a nice way to add something different to my day? I need to snap out of autopilot mode and mindfully interact with people, even during my commute.

Whatever the cause of this feeling that time is flying by more quickly than ever, it gives me more reason to take in every moment, make it count, and be present to every day of my life.

I had a nice morning. Both boys were awake so I had lots of cuddles and kisses in bed. Todd got me a nice card and made my birthday memorable by planning a meal and get-together with my family on the weekend. I am one lucky girl.

Presence. Gratitude. Love

Monday, July 20 – Let the moment seize you

It's a warm, slightly muggy morning following an extremely hot and muggy weekend.

On Saturday evening, Todd and I watched a great movie called *Boyhood*, which my mom recommended after seeing it at the Toronto International Film Festival (TIFF). It follows a boy's life from little kid to adolescent, a reminder of how fast childhood years go by. I really liked a line at the end of the movie when a girl says, "You know how the saying goes, 'Seize the moment'? I think it's kind of backwards. Aren't the moments seizing us?" The main character muses about how many moments there are and agrees. I interpret this line as meaning that we don't control nearly as much about our lives as we think. In my little bubble, it may feel like events revolve around my decisions, but there's a great big world out there that's totally out of my control. Perhaps the key is to accept this and let the moments seize me by staying present to each one. Otherwise, those moments might pass me by.

This must be an important lesson, as I found two powerful quotes with the same message from visionaries I admire:

> *We had to learn ourselves and, further, we had to teach the despairing men, that it did not really matter what we expected from life, but rather what life expected from us.*
>
> —Viktor E. Frankl, *Man's Search for Meaning*

> *Instead of asking, "What do I want from life?" a more powerful question is, "What does life want from me?"*
>
> —Eckhart Tolle

I will meditate on these thoughts for a while.

Let Go.

Tuesday, July 21 – Look good, feel good

I had a slow start to the morning as I slept in, then had a hard time deciding what to wear. I'm getting bored with my clothes. Perhaps it's time to renew my closet.

I did a major wardrobe refresh not long after Austin was born, a "Mommy Makeover" offered by an image consultant I met at my mommy meetup group. The three-month makeover included a colour analysis, personality and body profiling, wardrobe assessment, and personal shopping trip. It was the best money I ever spent, a major transformation in my life. I know it may not be everyone's cup of tea, but for me, it really was.

Before the Mommy Makeover, I went about my clothes shopping as I did in other areas of my life, from the practical, logical perspective of the accountant in me. This approach didn't result in a lot of inspired or flattering choices. I bought a lot of black, because doesn't everything go with black? I was a sucker for sales and good deals. Yes, I did gravitate toward some colours that suited me. But for the most part, I wore mostly dark, boring, practical clothes and shoes that worked "okay" for my weird, wide feet, but were usually less than stylish. I looked frumpy because I disregarded my body type. And I definitely didn't like shopping. I never knew what to look for, so I wasted a lot of time. Most of my shopping would happen in big spurts at outlet malls, just to get it out of the way.

Fast forward to after the Mommy Makeover: I've learned that when I look good, I feel good. I have a colourful wardrobe, void of any black at all (navy blue, grey, and dark brown are my base colours). I carry my colour palette with me when I go shopping (Clear—a mix of Spring and Winter), and I actually enjoy the process. I can pop in and out of stores on my lunch break at work and know immediately if there are clothes that suit me. I shop smart, still on the lookout for a good deal, but with confidence. I can also splurge on clothes that I love. Before I purchase something, I ask myself, *Do I love it?* Marie Kondo's first principle for tidying the home applies here: *Does it bring me joy?*

Her approach is useful for all kinds of decision-making, now that I think of it. What brings me joy? What people bring me joy?

It's a cloudy morning with a bit of rain, so it's quite dreary outside. Sometimes the weather sets the tone for the day. Todd and I had to sprint for the train, so now I'm hot, sweaty, and sticky with frizzy hair. What did I just say about looking good and feeling good? Ha.

Intention. Presence.

Monday, August 17 – Stay-at-home parenting

I just met up with girlfriends I used to work with at my first post-university job at an accounting firm. It's been a while since we got together, and it was wonderful to catch up. Sylvia and Alana recently bought new houses, and Tara just decided to become a stay-at-home mom with her three kids. That was always what I thought I'd do if I somehow ended up with three children. After two kids, I don't know that I'd have the capacity to continue working full-time while providing the support, attention and guidance they need. It was a tough decision for Tara, but a rewarding one. She had to follow her heart. I have many other friends who've made the same choice, and it's never easy. After many years of schooling, it may seem like "wasted" education, but I think it's quite the opposite. Education will never be a waste, as it will make for better mothers, people, partners, community helpers, and so on. These roles can be just as important as those at paid places of work.

Todd has been playing around with the idea of being a stay-at-home dad. One concern that comes up for him is about how this would be perceived by others. I think this kind of worry is natural, but shouldn't guide our decisions. A helpful thing to remember is that life is fluid—decisions we make today aren't necessarily permanent. It may turn out that after Tara's children reach a certain age, she'll choose to return to the workforce. Perhaps she'll get a part-time job or become an entrepreneur. Perhaps she'll find that she loves being a stay-at-home parent and is satisfied with running a household and caring for children full-time.

And then there's Josa, who's trying to balance her busy work hours with her family life. It isn't easy, especially in the financial services industry. Work culture and expectations are hard to shift. I face a similar challenge. Sometimes it feels like the world is trying to pull me along a certain path; the pressure to conform to societal norms is so strong. I have to be a maverick, stand my own ground and follow my own path, do what's best for me. As Brené Brown writes in her book, *Brave the Wilderness*, "braving the wilderness" is being true to myself and acting authentically, even when it goes against what society expects of me, even when I have critics and naysayers.[42]

I am thankful for longtime friends.

Let Go. Intention. Purpose. Balance. Gratitude.

Monday, August 31 – Time for change

Back to my regular commute and work routine. I'm starting to feel that my journal entries will be much the same from day to day. I suppose every day is a wee bit different, and over time, I'll recognize and appreciate the differences.

Yesterday was such an ordinary day, but it struck me as a perfectly ordinary day. It started out with coffee on the patio, followed by haircuts for all three boys. This is a hobby and creative outlet that

I have taken up. I find it enjoyable, not to mention economical and practical, to cut the boys' hair myself. I learned from YouTube tutorials, and of course practice. Austin's hair is not forgiving; we still have a laugh about a cut I gave him one holiday season that we call the 'Lloyd Christmas Christmas cut', after the *Dumb and Dumber* movie character played by Jim Carrey. After the haircuts, I did a dance workout in the basement, helped the boys with their homework, and made some progress on my online Cub Scout leader training. We then ran some errands. Such a regular day, complete with getting frustrated with the boys as they ran around Costco and Subway.

The big news for our family is that Todd made his decision and officially told his director last week that he'd like to take a year off to take care of the boys full-time. He hasn't been particularly happy with his job for the last little while. I don't think he minds the work, but he isn't really passionate about it. He designs tax legislation, but his true love is programming. His plan is to take computer-related courses while he is off with the boys. It will be a big change for our family. We'll lose our nanny but gain a stay-at-home dad. I'll lose my commuting buddy, and with that, our daily quiet time together. With change comes a little anxiety, as our life is pretty good right now, and we'll be moving onto a new path. It reminds me of a quote I came across recently:

> *We can't be afraid of change. You may feel very secure in the pond that you are in, but if you never venture out of it, you will never know that there is such a thing as an ocean, a sea. Holding onto something that is good for you now may be the very reason why you don't have something better.*
>
> —C. JoyBell C.

It's time for us to step out of our secure pond and perhaps discover an ocean. It's a warm late summer morning, the last week before school starts. As I enjoy my morning coffee, I notice that the train is slightly busier this morning. People must be getting back from their summer holidays. Today I am thankful for ordinary days, warm summer mornings, and my commuting buddy. But I'm also grateful for the opportunity for change and discovery.

Presence. Balance. Gratitude.

Friday, September 4 – Giving

It's another warm, muggy morning that feels much more like the middle of summer than the beginning of September. We have one last long weekend, and then it's back to school for the kids.

While I am thankful for so much—our country, my family's health, friends, a satisfying career—my heart is heavy this morning, thinking about people who are struggling around the world. Lately, my Facebook feed is full of stories that remind me that so many are faced with immense challenges:

Refugees fleeing Syria by watercraft, searching for safety. The heartbreaking picture of a toddler who looks so much like a little Austin, his body being carried out of the sea after his family's small boat capsized.

Friends fundraising to support childhood stroke research. Their son was born with a condition that was unknown at the time, and they are now faced with the everyday reality of raising a child with a disability.

And the homeless people I walk past on my way to work, begging for change, each with an untold story. Is it mental health challenges that got the best of them due to insufficient government, community, or family support? Perhaps addiction issues resulting from a challenging upbringing or misdirection at some point in their life?

If I am not mindful, I can slip down a dark path in my mind, consumed by negativity and sadness. But if I am mindful, these stories serve as a wake-up call. They're reminders not to take my life for granted. I pause and consider what I can do to help others in need. From moment to moment, I might play the role of a person who needs help or one who provides it. I want to be awake to which I am, in that moment, receiver or giver. They're both important roles.

Charitable giving is very important to me, whether it's for the community United Way, the Canadian Red Cross, or causes that friends and family are raising money for. It's a form of sharing. There are so many ways to give, not just financially. I can give my time, my energy, and simply, my love. Right now, I will try to think of simple things to give.

Austin has discovered the joy of giving. Last night, he was busy making a present for Carter: a Lego Scarlet Witch minifigure. He was so happy when he gave it to Carter this morning.

> *When we give cheerfully and accept gratefully, everyone is blessed.*
>
> —Maya Angelou

Gratitude. Presence.

Friday, September 11 – Six Elements of Wellness

It's a beautiful, sunny morning. The temperature has finally dropped a bit. We had heat warnings over the long weekend with temperatures up to 40°C.

We had a wellness session at work in which a woman from a company called Organized to the Max talked to us about balance. She introduced a Balance Wheel that includes six dimensions, or life areas:

- Social & Cultural,
- Financial & Career,
- Physical & Health,
- Mental & Education,
- Ethical & Spiritual,
- Family & Home.

I think we all have different thresholds for each dimension, but a minimum must be met to have a healthy, balanced, and happy life. Lately, the Social & Cultural dimension has been lacking for me. We haven't made any plans, and I haven't spent a lot of time with friends. Before I went back to working five days a week, I volunteered regularly at the boys' school. Plus, we used to attend church on most Sundays, where I volunteered as a Sunday school teacher. This met my social needs as well as spiritual. Since we've stopped going to church, there's been a gap in the social and spiritual dimensions for me.

I think I need to be more accepting, gentle, and kind to myself. I like to aim for perfection, which of course is impossible to attain, and makes it hard to feel satisfied and happy. The Cub Scout motto "Do Your Best" really resonates with me. It's simple yet sound advice that's simultaneously freeing and grounding. I shall not aim for perfection, but aim to do my best!

Perhaps at this point in my life, the Social & Cultural dimension will be unbalanced, but at another point I'll have an opportunity to spend more time with community and friends, and it'll balance out in the bigger picture.

Regardless, I'm grateful for all areas of my life. I will make an effort to stay present to every moment and appreciate it. I will be confident that I'm doing the best that I can. I will take advantage of opportunities to balance different facets of my life, and combine a few when I can. If I go for a walk with a friend on a trail and pick up garbage along the way, I'd be touching on multiple elements: social, cultural, physical health, spiritual (being in nature), and financial (saving money, as a walk is free entertainment). I love incorporating efficiency with intention, mindfulness, and balance.

Balance. Do Your Best. Intention. Gratitude.

Wednesday, September 23 – New beginnings

It's a foggy, grey morning, and quite mild. Despite the drab weather, as I drove to the train station, sipping my coffee and noticing the quiet stillness around us—just a few dog walkers and a small lineup of cars at the McDonald's drive-thru—I couldn't help but say to Todd, "I just love mornings." And I do. I love the newness and freshness of the day, with its untapped potential. It's my favourite time of day. Perhaps it's also the feeling of closeness to my true self, since I've so recently emerged from the rejuvenation of sleep. My mind is rested and hasn't had much of a chance to step in and mess things up. Mornings are a new beginning that we get to experience every day. As Thich Nhat Hanh says, "Waking up this morning, I smile. Twenty-four brand new hours are before me. I vow to live fully in each moment and to look at all beings with eyes of compassion."

I start my day with the warm memory of the silhouette of an eight-year-old in the doorway, waving goodbye as we pull out of the driveway. A morning send-off, topping off sweet hugs and loving kisses, that leaves me smiling.

I led my first Cub Scout meeting last night. Another new beginning to add to the Social & Cultural dimension and help balance my life further. Carter seemed to enjoy it, although he was very tired by the end of the night. He wanted me to spend more time with him and his group, not the others. I'll miss it when the boys are older and want little to do with their parents, especially in front of their friends. I relish the fact that he likes having me around now.

Lots of new beginnings for all of us this fall, as Carter is taking hip-hop classes and Austin is starting soccer with Todd as his coach. I'm thankful for our health, which allows us to participate in activities and take on responsibilities we enjoy.

Gratitude. Balance. Presence.

Friday, October 16 – The future is uncertain, so enjoy today

The days are getting shorter. It's around half past seven and the sun has not yet risen. A soft orange glow along the horizon shows that it's coming along, but lazily so.

I've been thinking a lot about Todd's dad, who is struggling with Parkinson's disease. He was diagnosed when he turned sixty-five, the year he retired from a long career at the local quarry. Beyond the friendships he had there, it was just a job to support his family, and he looked forward to retiring. He dreamed of buying a horse and travelling to Nova Scotia to visit family and friends. Now, he doesn't have the health or the energy to enjoy the projects he'd envisioned for his retirement.

This is a lesson for me to live life in the moment and not put anything off until another time, like when I retire. There are no guarantees for what the future holds, so it's important to enjoy each moment, each day.

Our train has unexpectedly stopped. I'll pause to enjoy the sun that has now emerged above the horizon and the birds perched in the trees, which have started losing their leaves.

Presence.

Tuesday, October 20 – Values and nature

It's a rainy, dark morning. I can only see a few lights shining in the darkness as we travel past. Todd and I are both tired this morning after an especially busy day yesterday.

Among our usual daily activities, I had a Cub Scout meeting. It was held outside at a local park. The evening was beautiful and mild, and the kids had a great time collecting sticks to build with and playing manhunt. Outdoor meetings are one of the things I love about Scouts. When I first registered Carter in the program, I mostly did it because his friends were in it. Even though I was in Girl Guides as a girl, the Scouts weren't really on my radar. The Guides may be one of those things I took for granted in my own childhood. The values that are taught in the program seemed like a given to me, but they aren't actually prevalent in public school. And yet, they're fundamental in developing emotionally intelligent, well-rounded people. It was only when I decided to volunteer as a Scout leader and did the many hours of online training that I realized what a wonderful program it is. Scouting is based on three broad principles:

- Duty to God: a person's relationship with the spiritual values of life, the fundamental belief in a force above mankind.
- Duty to others: a person's relationship with, and responsibility within, society in the broadest sense of the term - his or her family, local community, country and the world at large, as well as respect for others and for the natural world.
- Duty to self: a person's responsibility to develop his or her own potential, to the best of that person's ability.[43]

Along with these values is a significant outdoors and adventure component. In fact, a certain proportion of meetings must be held outdoors.

I think I've underestimated the value of nature in my life. Living in Canada in the winter, I can easily go for days without stepping outside when it's cold. This is especially true for those of us who work downtown Toronto, where underground tunnels directly connect much of the financial district to the subway and commuter trains. With the rise in prominence of technology in our lives, nature seems like a forgotten gem, even though it has such rejuvenating wellness qualities. It brings me closer to who I really am. Eckhart Tolle eloquently describes the power of nature in *Stillness Speaks*:

> We depend on nature not only for our physical survival. We also need nature to show us the way home, the way out of the prison of our own minds. We got lost in doing, thinking,

remembering, anticipating—lost in a maze of complexity and a world of problems.

We have forgotten what rocks, plants, and animals still know.

We have forgotten how to be—to be still, to be ourselves, to be where life is: Here and Now.[44]

I am so grateful for nature, for democracy and freedom in our country, and for the people.

Purpose. Balance. Do Your Best. Presence. Gratitude.

Wednesday, November 25 – Play

It's a cold November morning. Boots and winter coats are out. The ground is covered with a white layer of frost, and the sun is a bright yellow-orange ball hanging low in the sky. The days are going by so fast and the to-do list is long. I've been contemplating applying for a term position in Basel, Switzerland for two years. Big decisions tend to take up a lot of space in my mind and add to my stress. I need to remember to . . .

Slow down.
Breathe.
Smile.
Prioritize.

Sometimes I want to jump off the hamster wheel for a second, just for a breather.

Last weekend was a bit like a breather. It was a change, anyway. I went camping with Carter and the Cub Scout group. We stayed in a heated lodge, so it was fairly comfortable. We spent a lot of time outdoors doing activities and free play time, which the kids spent building forts in the forest. It was fun to get into playing with them, helping them roll logs into place for their forts. It brought back memories of the freedom and fun of being a kid. Play is great for everyone.

I will try to regularly incorporate play into my day. Dancing along to *Just Dance* video games is a kind of play I love to do. It makes me happy, gives me exercise, improves my reflexes, and makes me feel like a kid again.

As George Bernard Shaw famously said, "We don't stop playing because we grow old; we grow old because we stop playing."

I'm thankful for a healthy body that enables me to do yoga, bike, walk, dance, and do all the activities that I enjoy.

Let Go. Balance. Presence. Gratitude.

Friday, November 28 – War and peace

There's a lot going on in the world around us. A couple of weeks ago, there were six simultaneous ISIS terrorist attacks in Paris that killed around 130 people. The attacks have garnered worldwide attention, and social media is full of comments and opinions. Some posts bring messages of love while others respond in fear or in hate. When I read hateful messages, especially without factual backing, I find myself tempted to argue back. In moments like these, I need to tap into my mindfulness practice. Heated reactions would probably only perpetuate the problem. Online conversations are difficult because there is so much context I lack. I don't know the people on the other side, and I can't see their facial reactions or hear their tone of voice. I can't really connect with them to understand where they're coming from. I have to wonder how likely it is that I can turn around their way of thinking by lashing out at them. I'll bet that there's a 99.9% chance that I won't. So what will I gain by adding an emotionally charged argument to the mix? Perhaps I could add value to the conversation if I contribute facts from reputable sources. But I'd have to be very cautious in stating an opposing opinion. I might consider how open I am to changing my opinion. If I'm not, it's likely that the other party isn't either. Constructive debates usually only happen between people who are open-minded and curious.

While I can't control much in the world around me, I can choose my mindset and my response.

Today, I'm praying for the world, sending peace into it. I'm thankful for what we have and for the messages of love being spread in this tumultuous time. This is what the world needs, not more fear and hate.

> *Darkness cannot drive out darkness; Only light can do that.*
> *Hate cannot drive out hate; Only love can do that.*
>
> —Martin Luther King, Jr.

Love. Gratitude.

Monday, January 4, 2016 – Purpose and vision

Happy New Year! It's a dark, cold January morning. The moon is a bright sliver set high in the sky. It seems more like nighttime, but there's something nice about it. I find an odd comfort in being up early and back to my routine after two weeks of Christmas holidays.

I'm not much for New Year's resolutions, as I try to live with purpose and intention on a daily basis. I don't want to wait for some arbitrary point in time to make changes if I feel that I need them. Right now, I need to come up with strategies to help me stay mindful and calm in my day-to-day life. Maybe yoga on Sundays would be a good thing to add to my schedule? There's a family class I could do with the boys.

I still feel the need to incorporate a regular spiritual practice into my life, something to remind me that there's something greater than me and to draw me toward my greater purpose. I should define my purpose and vision more clearly. In the corporate world, running an organization without articulating a vision or mission statement would be quite detrimental to its success. An effective mission statement acknowledges key factors for success in the environment they are operating in. As an individual, I benefit from crafting my own personal vision, too. I can ask myself: What's my goal? What differentiates me? What are my values? What's important to me?

Without defining the answers to these questions, I may end up directionless and get caught up in tasks that don't actually align with my goals. In this era of constant connection through social media, advertising, and all the people around me, there are constant demands on my attention (and money). I may unintentionally prioritize things that others value, but that don't bring me fulfilment. If I do define my personal vision, I'll be able to refer to it to make decisions with purpose and intention. This is a fundamental factor in creating a happy and fulfilled life.

I'm a to-do list type of person. My daily to-do list now includes not only chores that need to get done, but also activities that bring joy and balance to my life—I intentionally make time for them. And it feels so good to cross them off the list! My weekend to-do list starts like this: coffee, meditation, seven-minute workout, play with the boys . . .

The sky is getting lighter and the moon is fading as the train rolls into Union Station.

Purpose. Intention. Presence.

Friday, January 8 - Impermanence

Yet another very dark January morning, but at least it's mild at -2°C.

Sadly, a colleague's father passed away this week from a heart attack. I find funerals can be a force for awakening, or questioning at least. Life happens and life can end unexpectedly. We just never know what will be thrown our way. It's another reminder to focus on what matters in life. The more flexible I am mentally, the more smoothly I'll ride the waves. It's a time when I am reminded that **I am not here on this earth forever—none of us are.** This is one commonality that we all have as humans: we will all die. This is simply a fact. I can't change this. What I can do is choose how to live my life. I can choose to live consciously, purposefully, with my eyes, mind, and heart wide open.

> *It is not impermanence that makes us suffer. What makes us suffer is wanting things to be permanent when they are not.*
>
> — Thich Nhat Hanh

Purpose. Presence. Intention.

Tuesday, January 12 – World balance

The snow has finally arrived for the winter. With a heavy cloud cover, it's dark this morning, with the exception of the soft glow of the fresh blanket of snow.

The boys went for a sleepover at their Nana and Grandpa's house while Todd and I had a date night. We went out for sushi and then to a movie: *The Big Short*, about the 2008 financial crisis. I found it extremely interesting, especially since I work in the banking industry. It made me think about the consequences of greed—what happens when individuals look out for their own interests at the expense of others'. In our society, it's seen as normal to covet power and wealth. Those who live in giant mansions with yachts and fancy vacation homes are put on pedestals as the "winners." But when our main goal is to get rich, other values are lost along the way. For every individual in the winners' circle, there are many, many people who struggle to get the basic essentials in life. How is that okay?

It reminds me of a story of children in an African tribe who are offered a bowl of treats by a tree. They are told that whoever gets to the bowl first gets to have all the treats. But instead of racing to the bowl to beat the others, the children all held hands and ran together to the treats. When they were asked why they did that, they replied, "How can one of us be happy if all the others are sad?"

This allegory illustrates the concept of *ubuntu*, an African philosophy of oneness emphasizing the interconnectedness of all life. This philosophy prioritizes the well-being of the group over the individual.

Sometimes it feels like western society is so far removed from that mindset.

I should think about what I'm putting value on in my life. How does this contribute to the world around me?

I pray for us. I pray for the world. I pray that we consider our connectedness and our responsibilities to one another. However small our individual role may seem, it is important.

Take care of ourselves. Take care of each other. Love one another. It is that simple.

Balance. Intention. Purpose. Love.

Friday, January 15 – The power of questions

It's a dark but mild January morning. January feels like the longest month of the year. The weeks go by so slowly. Even though it's only mid-January, it seems like Christmas and the winter break were ages ago.

It's my good friend Kelly's fortieth birthday today. The wave of fortieth birthdays for my group of friends has begun. It's triggering a lot of questions for me, and I think for my friends as well. I feel the temptation to judge this milestone. Am I old? Is this midlife? Have I done what I wanted in my life so far? Is this where I thought I would be at this age?

Questions can be very powerful. They give me the opportunity to pause. To reflect. To assess. To recalibrate.

I ask questions for a living, and it never ceases to amaze me how powerful simple questions can be. Important insights are uncovered by good questions, especially when they're asked with the right intentions and genuine curiosity. They bring truth and knowledge to light.

And so, at this milestone I say, bring on the questions. But leave the judgments behind. Leave out the unnecessary expectations fabricated many years ago by myself or others. This milestone is an opportunity for introspection. Hopefully, there will be no big surprises. But if there are, I will be thankful that I have the courage to ask these questions now. I will set intentions and take action as needed.

Purpose. Intention. Let Go.

Tuesday, February 23 – Phud

I'm on a later train again this morning. I know I have a late afternoon meeting and will get home later tonight, so I chose to have breakfast with the boys.

We had a nice weekend. The boys slept over at Nana and Grandpa's, and Todd and I went out for dinner and then to Kristin's fortieth birthday celebration. All the wine and food I consumed totally negated the yoga I did with Nicole in the morning and the past week's workouts. I've been trying to lose the winter "phud." I totally made up that word as I don't know what else to call it—the winter phase that my body goes through where it craves carbs (perhaps to build up an extra layer to keep warm). The weather makes it harder to get outside for the usual exercise of the warmer months. So the cycle begins: eat more, exercise less. The extra weight that comes with it is what I call the "phud." I need to break free of the phud. It's even more important to stay present in these months to avoid getting sucked into the phud cycle. Once I'm in, it's like swimming against the current. I've been consciously trying to get myself out of there: going for a walk during lunch, seven-minute workouts at night, and yoga. Yoga really helps with body awareness and staying present.

Presence. Intention.

Thursday, March 24 – Connection

Today is a snow day, or more accurately, a freezing rain day. The schools in the area are closed and public transportation is cancelled. After spending a week in consistently sunny and warm weather in the Caribbean, Canada is feeling like a bit of an adventure. Every day is different; you never know what weather you're going to get. If I don't check the forecast in the morning before going out, I could end up completely ill-prepared and uncomfortable. These days, it might be cold, warm, rainy, snowy, windy—you name it, you could get it.

Our March break trip to Grenada was fantastic, a welcome reprieve from unpredictable Canadian weather. We thoroughly enjoyed our time on the island: the resort we stayed at, the people we met, the food, the swimming and snorkeling, the entire adventure. We took in a CONCACAF soccer game played by a Canadian women's under-18 team and hung out with a lovely family from London, Ontario. We found that we had quite a bit in common with them. They own a marketing business and work hard, but also value family time. We talked about the book *The 4-Hour Workweek* by Tim Ferriss, which inspires them. They try to maximize their efficiency so that they can carve time out of their business schedule to travel and enjoy life. They're usually able to book three trips per year.

Hanging out with that family made me realize that people are what makes me enjoy experiences. Life is all about connection. Austin just loved Maya, who's nine years old, and kept asking about her. Carter was more cool and aloof, although I could tell he enjoyed hanging out with her. He especially liked playing the piano with her.

The island has a population of just over 100,000 people, so it has a friendly small-town feel. It's also one of the world's largest producers of nutmeg. I'm so thankful for my opportunity to travel, explore, meet new people, and spend a lot of time with my family.

Gratitude. Balance. Let Go.

Friday, April 1 – *Prisoner of Tehran*

It's a dull, grey morning, but I can see a hint of sunshine peeking out through the dark clouds. We had a thunderstorm last night. There's something about a thunderstorm that reminds me that we don't have control over everything, if anything, really.

I've been a little tired this week as I stayed up late a few nights to finish the book *Prisoner of Tehran*. It's a well-written memoir of an Iranian woman's experience living in Iran during the revolution in the 1970s–80s. When the Islamic government came into power, citizens got arrested for giving their opinions if they contradicted the government's. Schools and universities were shut down while they overhauled the education system. They replaced teachers with political Islamic fundamentalists who didn't necessarily know much about the subjects they were teaching. Western literature was banned. At the time of this writing, the population of Iran is about seventy-eight million people.

Today, I'm particularly grateful to live in Canada, for the education system, freedom, democracy, and relative peace. I love being surrounded by a diverse population of people from all around the world. I love learning about different cultures and ways of life.

Gratitude.

Thursday, April 21 – Judgments: good/bad

It's a cool spring morning. Clouds are just covering the sun, which is promising to emerge.

A lot has happened in the last couple of weeks. My sister Janice had surgery on April 14th to remove a cyst on her ovary. For Janice, any operation is a little more complicated due to the scar tissue from previous surgeries, her heart condition, and internal defibrillator. She is a beacon of strength and has overcome so many physical health challenges, especially considering she's only in her thirties.

Janice has a history of health issues that started when she was three years old. She was born without the muscle that controls the flow of urine from the bladder, which required multiple corrective procedures and surgeries. Later, when she and Steve were ready to start a family, she discovered her fallopian tubes were blocked and needed to be removed, so she was unable to carry a child. Steve's sister volunteered to be a surrogate for them and successfully carried their daughter, Delainey. Janice took domperidone so she could breastfeed, but experienced an episode with her heart, which led to the discovery that she has a life-threatening heart arrhythmia. Thank goodness for science and modern medicine, as her defibrillator implant keeps her safe.

And now, here we are, dealing with her latest health challenge. I drove to the hospital with my mom and met Steve there to wait while Janice was in surgery. Steve's mom and dad came a little bit later and brought Delainey with them, so we all waited together. When the doctor came out of surgery and took Steve into a small room beside the waiting area, I was so nervous I probably wasn't breathing. I thought I overheard the doctor say "laparoscopy," which kind of confused me. As far as we knew, a laparoscopy wasn't an option due to Janice's scar tissue, though it would have been less invasive than open surgery. So when Steve came out of the room, barely holding back a smile, and told us that the doctor had indeed successfully removed the cyst via laparoscope, I can't tell you how ecstatic I felt. We were all in shock at the news.

I'm hesitant to label the results of the procedure as good or bad, as who knows what series of events will happen in life? What may seem like good news today may end up feeling like bad news tomorrow. I will try not to label things as good or bad, but rather, accept them as they are.

I really like the saying "It is what it is." One of my old bosses used to say it all the time, and it makes a lot of sense. **Accept what life throws my way and deal with it without judgment.**

Mindfulness instructor Tamara Levitt from the Calm meditation app recites a story that aptly illustrates this concept. It goes like this . . .

> One night, a farmer's horse ran away. The neighbours said to him, "What terrible luck that is. How unfortunate for you!"

"Maybe," said the farmer.

The next day, the farmer's horse returned with two other wild horses. The neighbours congratulated him, saying, "What great fortune!"

"Maybe," said the farmer.

The day after that, the farmer's son was riding one of the untamed horses and fell off. He broke his leg and would forever limp. "How awful!" the neighbours exclaimed.

"Maybe," said the farmer.

Shortly after, the army came through the town, looking for able-bodied men to fight in a war. Seeing the farmer's son limping, they passed him by. "How lucky you are!" said the neighbours.

"Maybe," said the farmer.[45]

I will take this news as it is and feel relief that the surgery was successful. I love my sister, and I was so happy and grateful to be there with her and her family.

Gratitude. Let Go.

Thursday, May 5 – Making people feel valued

It's still a little cool in the morning, but I can sense that spring is on its way.

It's been a pretty busy week. The best part of my morning yesterday was volunteering in Austin's class. I read a book to the kids, which they really enjoyed. Because I've been there so often, I now know the kids by name. It's amazing to see how they light up when I call them by name. I can tell it makes them feel very special. We learn so many basics of human behaviour with children, and this is a good example. As humans, all we really want is to feel important. From my experience, simple ways to make people feel valued are:

- Say their name.
- Make eye contact with them.
- Truly listen to them when they talk.
- Smile at them.

These are not difficult at all, but can have a hugely positive impact on our relationships. And I'm not the only person who thinks so. Branding expert Andris Pone writes in his book, *Attract: Power Up Your One-of-a-Kind Personal Brand*, "Through years of working with individuals and organizations on their brands, a vital core belief took shape: that **ultimately what we want as humans is to be valued by others** [emphasis mine]. It is this appreciation that gives meaning to our lives."[46] And In Oprah and Deepak Chopra's guided meditation *21-Day Meditation Experience: Perfect Health*, Oprah tells us, "We are all seeking that spirit-to-spirit connection that enables us to feel seen and heard. That's one of the things I learned in all the years of the Oprah show, that that's the number one common denominator in the human experience—we all want to know that we are seen and heard."[47]

I will try to keep this in mind in all my interactions, including at work, and consider how I'm making the other person feel. I know that when I don't feel valued, I start feeling defensive and respond in a reactive way. Making others feel valued can vastly impact leadership effectiveness and success in life in general. People are what make the world go round.

Love. Purpose. Presence.

Thursday, May 26 – The pure presence of children

Mmm, some days coffee really hits the spot, warms me up, makes me smile, and soothes my soul. This is one of those days for me. It's a warm but rainy morning with thunderstorms expected throughout the day.

I got a taste of the presence and awareness of children the other day thanks to Carter. I was helping him floss his teeth when I noticed him gazing dreamily out of the bathroom window. I asked him what he was thinking about, expecting him to answer, "Imagining what my Disney Infinity character would look like if I invented one," or "Deadpool battling bad guys," or something along those lines. But no! Instead, he said, "I'm looking at the shapes in the tree leaves like I always do. I see a dragon. It's a perfectly shaped dragon. And I see a helicopter."

He wasn't lost in thought at all, but focused on what was right in front of him. In that moment.

I took note and feel grateful for another teachable moment from my son.

Presence. Gratitude.

Friday, June 25 – The things I love

It's a beautiful morning, the sun shining high and bright, not a cloud in the sky from my view out of the GO train window. The sky is such a pale blue colour, it almost looks white, with just a subtle hint of orange along the horizon.

I watched a great episode of Super Soul Sunday that included Eckhart Tolle and Dr. Shefali. How influential these two people have been in my life. And Oprah too, of course, who's brought outstanding people into my life in one way or another. I am happy.

I thought it would be nice to make a list of things that I love, that inspire me, that make my heart soar, that have helped shape my life. Here goes, off the top of my head and in no particular order . . .

> My parents, my sisters, my brother, Todd, my boys, my friends, the boys' teachers, their preschool, *The 7 Habits of Highly Effective People*, *A New Earth*, *The Conscious Parent*, Oprah, Adele, The Killers, the song "Hallelujah," the song "Over the Rainbow" as sung by IZ, my town, hikes, trails, my bike, our house, my elliptical machine, *Just Dance*, the seven-minute workout app, my Fitbit, kickboxing, our firepit, camping, MacGregor Point Provincial Park, my childhood house and property, my extended family, my cousins Emily and Laura, wine, the radio station Funny 820 AM, Lululemon, so many books—*A House in the Sky, The Invention of Wings, Lean In, The Shack*, Corry (nurse at the ICU in the hospital where Carter was born), prenatal yoga, prenatal classes, yoga classes, Julia (yoga instructor), Janelle Long (image consultant), Grenada, the Dominican Republic, Cuba, the ocean, Ivey Business School, the GO train, my boss, so many of my co-workers, my work, my childhood church, God, Canada, the song "Danza Kuduro", coffee, mornings . . .

We all have our own lists, and they grow over time. It's fun to take the time to take stock of these gifts, to get swept away in a wave of gratitude.

Love. Gratitude.

Monday, July 18 – Happy 40th to me!

It's a gorgeous summer morning. The sun is already high in a cloudless sky. I'm settling back to work this week after a two-week vacation.

Vacations are wonderful for stirring us up, shaking us out of our routine, and giving us an opportunity to reflect on what we want out of life. It was after our vacation in Cuba that Todd decided to take a year off work. As for me, I'd been contemplating applying for a promotion. But I had an "Aha" moment where I realized that I preferred to stay in my current position, that I didn't need to be in a big hurry to get to the next level. I should enjoy the role I'm in, the people I work with, and the challenges and opportunities it offers.

I love my position for a lot of reasons, but a big one is that I so enjoy working with people in a leadership role, empowering them to be their best and reach their highest potential. Our organization has the mandate to protect depositors' money, which serves the public, so I feel like I'm making a meaningful contribution in my career.

Another big bonus is that it leaves room for other things in my life that give me satisfaction and make me happy: volunteering at the boys' schools and with Carter's Cub Scout group, working out and getting exercise, and having play time with the boys at the end of the day.

On the weekend, I celebrated my fortieth birthday with friends and family. I'm thankful for my forty years' journey so far. I have wonderful friends, wonderful family, an amazing husband, and inspiring children. I live in a great country, surrounded by many great people. So, I'm thankful for my life situation.

But most importantly, I'm thankful for my life: my ever-increasing moments of mindful awareness and happiness in my daily life; my ability to recognize my feelings and know when I need to pause and take in a mindful breath. I feel gratitude and love in an ever-increasing manner, for myself and for others. Forty to me is confidence, contentment, friends, family, intention, gratitude, and balance.

> *You are allowed to be both a masterpiece and a work in progress simultaneously.*
>
> —Sophia Bush

This is Life. What a gift.

Awake: My Happiness Formula

You find peace not by rearranging the circumstances of your life, but by realizing who you are at the deepest level.

—Eckhart Tolle

Here I am, over five years after writing my first journal entry. While the differences I feel in my life and my sense of inner peace are profound, from the outside, you wouldn't likely notice much of a change. I have the same job, the same family and friends, the same house. But the subtle differences shine through from the inside out. The confidence and happiness I feel can be seen in my smile, how I deal with life's challenges, and how I relate to others. My relationships are deeper; I feel more connected to many people in my life.

At work, colleagues comment that I always seem calm. This is because I am grounded in my leadership vision, which is based on compassion, authenticity, being my best, and empowering others to be their best too. I am able to approach my work with energy and engagement, doing what I can to support the organization's mandate.

And at home? I surveyed my family members on what differences they've seen in me over the last five years.

Todd responded that I'm less type A, less perfectionist, more happy and relaxed.

Austin, who is now ten years old, couldn't comment on my before-and-after since he was so young when I started journaling, so he just described me as a mom: I am a good mom who likes to hug; I let him make cookies; I drive him places; I do stuff with him. He also mentioned that I get exercise and I'm not on Facebook all day.

Carter, who is now twelve, reported: I'm more patient; I don't jump to conclusions as often; I think stuff through more; I'm calmer; I'm more open to others' ideas; it looks like I enjoy life more. He also said that I enjoy the outdoors and that I'm able to relax instead of being preoccupied. In his view, I'm definitely happier. I asked him what he thought the difference would be if I hadn't started practising mindfulness. His response was that we'd all be more stressed out since I'd be stressed out. He added that **everyone should practise mindful awareness because you become happier and everyone around you becomes happier.** This is seriously the best commendation I could ask for.

In the last few years, our family has found a flow that is much more serene, supportive, and respectful. Todd and I relate to each other as true partners. When one of us gets off-balance, we communicate it in a nonconfrontational way and work it out together. We rarely raise our voices at each other, if at all. He's been a stay-at-home dad for over four years now. Almost every day, we give appreciation for each other and the role each of us plays in our partnership and family. I know the work he does around the house—cooking, cleaning, organizing play dates, and so on—allows me to focus on my job and do the best I can in my career. He acknowledges that because of the work I do, our family is financially comfortable. We are able to save up for the boys' education and enroll them in the activities that they enjoy.

Todd is thriving in his new role, which has afforded him the opportunity to take up challenges like managing Austin's baseball team, learning a number of computer programming languages, and doing freelance website jobs. When he is happy and fulfilled, it flows into our relationship, as it does the other way around. We still have healthy debates as we don't always see eye to eye, but we appreciate the different perspective the other brings to the issue.

My relationships with Carter and Austin have also benefited from my mindfulness journey. I make it a habit to be as present as I can with them after work. Since I'm satisfied with the focus and time that I give at the office, I'm free to give my boys my full attention when I get home. Once I step through the door, it's my time with them and Todd.

My mindfulness practice has taught me to slow down and listen more closely. With the boys especially, I've learned that less talk and more presence from me is good for them. When I'm able to stay mindful with them, I pass along the insights I gain to diffuse conflict and maintain harmony. The four of us were out for a walk one morning, and Austin almost immediately started in with a litany of complaints: "My foot is sore. Why do we always have to do the things you want to do? Can we go back?" My first annoyed thought was, *How does this energetic kid get tired out so fast on a walk when he can play baseball for hours?* But rather than rebut his numerous complaints and feed into the negativity, I stepped back, listened, and said, "Austin, it's not like you to be so negative. Did you sleep well last night?"

"Yes," he said.
"Did you have breakfast this morning?"
"Well, no," he admitted. It was 10:30 am and he had been up since 7.

"Ah, that makes sense," I said. "You're probably hangry. Let's go home and get you some food." Just like that, the complaining stopped. We walked back to the house while he and Carter happily chatted.

I maintain my goal of raising the boys to be confident, happy individuals. My main objectives are to make them feel valued and to foster inner peace. They are each such unique and special people, and I aim to honour their hobbies and goals. Austin is a natural athlete and enjoys playing baseball and hockey. While

Carter also likes these sports, he has found his passion in filmmaking and video editing. He keeps himself busy with short film and special effect projects for his YouTube channel (carter d films). Most importantly, when I ask the boys how happy they are on a scale of one to ten, Austin says ten, and Carter says eight. That is very satisfying for me.

After taking a break to write this book, I have returned to journaling periodically. It happens naturally when I'm inspired to write. My entries often look very different now, with short, concise sentences. They aren't really stories anymore. Perhaps I no longer need to fully describe a situation to clarify to myself what's going on, and I can more easily skip the drama that I used to get caught up in. I'm much more aware of the external nature of situations I face and the things I don't have control over. I use labels to identify the thoughts that arise so that I can put more focus on letting them go. (This doesn't mean that difficult circumstances don't bother me or that feelings don't arise while I'm dealing with them. Sometimes it does help to methodically write through a challenge.)

Here's an example of a recent journal entry. There was a lot going on that day and I was struggling with a busy mind:

March 6, 2020

> It's Friday. Grey skies. Mind full. Grateful for all the people, ambitions, challenges, work, projects, and tasks that create the fullness. Accepting. Letting the past and future go. Settling into the present. Breathe. Trees. Birds. Let the thoughts roll by. Vacation planning. Birthdays, cards, gifts. Leadership issues—how to address. Meetings. Mentoring—lost job, career advice. Parenting—bad dreams, giving

confidence, hockey playoffs. Author—promotion strategy, publishing plan.

I also continue to practise mindful awareness daily. It's my ticket to waking up to happiness and inner peace, not to mention sharing those benefits with the people around me. I must include the disclaimer that I am not perfectly mindful at all times. But I do have many more moments of mindful awareness than I used to. This is a path I expect—and hope—to travel on for the rest of my life. It's a perfectly imperfect journey.

How I Woke Up to Happiness in My Daily Life

Each day of your life *is* your life. Make it count. Here's my formula for true happiness and inner peace:

Happiness = Presence + Gratitude + Intention + Balance + Do Your Best + Let Go + Love

- *Presence:* Being present in each moment.

  > This is where it all starts—mindful awareness. I believe that our natural state as humans is to be happy, but happiness gets clouded by our busy minds. Once I'm able to get past the thoughts and stories my mind creates, the feeling that remains is serene. I can access it whenever I put my intention on settling into the present moment, to leave space for connecting with the deeper "me" (rather than the surface "me," the ego). With practice, it has become easier to bring awareness to my thoughts without identifying with them or getting caught up in them. Unhealthy thought patterns like replaying past events and worrying about the future have less of a hold on me. I literally smell the roses, using my five senses to take in everyday moments and experience the

beauty of my surroundings. Just as importantly, I acknowledge my efforts and give myself appreciation for keeping up the practice.

- *Gratitude:* Being thankful on a daily basis for what I have and who I am.

As we've already heard, gratitude has the power to literally rewire the brain to experience happiness. By practising it daily, I train my brain to focus on the good in my life. Instead of trying hard to be a glass half-full type of person, I naturally and effortlessly see the full part of my metaphoric glass.

- *Purpose:* Building a vision and being clear on my values.

I have identified my north star—my guiding principles. By laying out my vision for who I want to be and what my core values are, I ensure that I'm spending my life focusing on what matters most to me. It helps me avoid getting tied up in less important tasks at the expense of my greater goals.

- *Intention:* Being intentional with my time, my attention, and my actions.

Once I have identified my guiding principles, I aim to live by them. I confidently set boundaries with myself (e.g., only after getting a certain amount of exercise can I indulge in watching TV) and with others (e.g., I don't accept being treated with disrespect). By acting with intention, I have less guilt and fewer regrets.

- *Balance:* Creating balance in each domain of my life.

I take care of my full self: mind, body, and spirit. Periodically, I remind myself of the six categories from the Balance Wheel: Social & Cultural, Financial & Career, Physical & Health, Mental & Education, Ethical & Spiritual, Family & Home.

I ask myself, *What category do I need to prioritize to bring better balance and alignment to my life?*

- *Do Your Best:* Aiming for the best I can be today (and not for perfection).

   "Do Your Best" is the Cub Scout motto, and it really is a good one. I do my best every day, knowing that my best will vary from day to day. I try not to aim for perfection anymore, as it hasn't served me well in the past. Life is about continuous learning, after all, not perfection. I feel satisfied if I can honestly say that I've tried my best today.

- *Let Go:* Accepting people and situations as they are. Letting go of expectations, judgments, and ego.

   Letting go of expectations. By accepting the circumstances I find myself in and setting aside my expectations of how others should behave or how events should unfold, I've eliminated a lot of unnecessary hard feelings, suffering, and drama.

   Letting go of judgments. By abandoning harsh judgments of others and of myself (I've been known to be my own worst critic), I've become more accepting and loving.

   Letting go of my ego. I try not to take myself too seriously or identify too closely with my life situation and physical body. I recognize that my true self is deeper than external factors and that my worth is not tied to my material form or my belongings.

- *Love:* Treating myself and others with kindness and compassion.

The real challenge was starting with loving myself. As the late British actor Robert Morley said, "To fall in love with yourself is the first secret to happiness."[48]

My formula is pretty simple, but does take continuous practice to live day by day. Changing mindset habits takes dedication and patience. But take heart: happiness is found in each moment, so all we need is a moment at a time.

Epilogue: Solid, Solid, Solid

Three years after starting my journal, I had the opportunity to attend a weekend retreat for women, an amazing getaway in which we were encouraged to try unfamiliar activities to push ourselves out of our comfort zones. One evening, we were treated to a group session with a spiritual healer. This kind of thing was entirely new to me, and I was intrigued. In a room of about a hundred women, the healer connected with the group, then had us centre ourselves and channel love. Anyone who wanted to connect with the spirit of a loved one was instructed to think about this individual. She walked around the room, pausing at certain people to connect with them. It was an incredible experience, to witness the impact she had on those women. The emotions were raw and intense, and I think very healing for many as old hurts and regrets were addressed.

The healer told us that we all had the ability to connect like this. Like anything else in life, it just takes practice. To demonstrate, she brought ten of us onstage, including me. We were partnered up with a stranger and asked to lend a personal item to our partner. I took off my watch and gave it to my partner, Jennifer. We were to hold the item closely and share what image, word, or thought came to us about its owner. When Jennifer was asked about me, holding my watch tightly, eyes closed, she said, "Solid, solid, solid." She added that she felt very secure and grounded, like she couldn't be moved out of place.

The healer turned to me, looked at me contemplatively, and asked, "Do you feel like you have everything you need in your life?"

Thinking not about my external life situation, but about what I had found inside of me, and with a certainty that was new to me, I took a deep, conscious breath and said:

"Yes, I do."

Acknowledgments

I am grateful to my wonderful parents, Marilyn and Bill, for the foundation and values they instilled in me. You allowed a love of life to flourish in me, which propels me forward in my endeavours. To my mom for your thoughtful counsel and edits.

To my siblings, Heather, Janice and Stu for always being there as lifelong allies. Thanks for reading my drafts and offering feedback and encouragement through the process.

Nicole Powrie, your constructive advice on the earliest version helped drive me forward. Not an easy task! I am thankful for your friendship and honesty.

The seed of my happiness formula started with a simple lunchtime conversation about life. I am grateful to Cherryl Persaud and Krista McMullen, my office and spiritual confidantes, for planting the kernel.

To Corry Nicholls for reviewing the manuscript in the midst of a busy life with a toddler and for your heartfelt feedback.

Thank you to my aunt, Lois Osborne, for your detailed edit and review. I could have written an entire chapter on resilience about you. Your humble strength was instrumental to Uncle Bert's remarkable story of awakening. And to Rebecca Hotham for your review and support for sharing your dad's story. You are both very special people.

For helping turn a dream into reality, I am indebted to my FriesenPress Editor. Your early, in-depth feedback gave me confidence. You understood me and helped transform my vision perfectly. Thank you to my whole FriesenPress team for holding my hand through the process, including Debbie Anderson and Mara Owusu.

Todd, where do I start? Your partnership, love and unending support has allowed me to be me. This book is our work. It wouldn't be possible without you stepping in with the boys and household duties to give me the opportunity to write. You provided valuable challenge, which sent me back to the drawing board a few times. You dared me to do my best. I love you.

And, finally to Carter and Austin. To each of you, thank you for being you. For being patient with me while I write and for letting me share our stories. I love you both to the moon and back (times infinity).

Notes

1 "Home > International Days > International Day of Happiness, 20 March", United Nations: Department of Economic and Social Affairs - Social Inclusion, accessed October 2020, https://www.un.org/development/desa/dspd/international-days/international-day-of-happiness.html

2 The Conference Board, "U.S. Job Satisfaction At Lowest Level In Two Decades," January 5, 2010, https://www.prnewswire.com/news-releases/us-job-satisfaction-at-lowest-level-in-two-decades-80699752.html

3 Martin E. P. Seligman, *Authentic Happiness: Using the New Positive Psychology to Realize Your Potential for Lasting Fulfillment* (New York: Free Press, 2002), 117.

4 Shawn Achor, *The Happiness Advantage: The Seven Principles of Positive Psychology That Fuel Success and Performance at Work* (New York: Currency, 2010), 8.

5 June De Vaus, Matthew J. Hornsey, Peter Kuppens, and Brock Bastian, "Exploring the East-West Divide in Prevalence of Affective Disorder: A Case for Cultural Differences in Coping With Negative Emotion," *Personality and social psychology review: an official journal of the Society for Personality and Social Psychology, Inc* 22(3) (August 2018): 85–304, https://doi.org/10.1177/1088868317736222.

6 Hannah Frishberg, "1 in 5 millennials are lonely and have 'no friends': survey," *New York Post*, August 2, 2019, https://nypost.com/2019/08/02/1-in-5-millennials-are-lonely-and-have-no-friends-survey/ .

7 Joan Bryden, "Coronavirus pandemic may spark an increase in mental-health struggles that could last years: study," *The Globe and Mail*, August 5, 2020, https://www.theglobeandmail.com/canada/

article-coronavirus-pandemic-may-spark-an-increase-in-mental-health-struggles/ .

8 *Merriam-Webster Dictionary*, "happiness (n.)," accessed August 2020, https://www.merriam-webster.com/dictionary/happiness.

9 Shefali Tsabary, *The Awakened Family: A Revolution in Parenting* (New York: Viking, 2016), 99.

10 Eckhart Tolle, *The Power of Now: A Guide to Spiritual Enlightenment* (Vancouver: Namaste Publishing, 1997), 68.

11 Courtney E. Ackerman, "What is Happiness and Why is it Important?", positivepsychology.com, 15-04-2020, https://positivepsychology.com/what-is-happiness/

12 Rick Hanson and Richard Mendius, *Buddha's Brain: The Practical Neuroscience of Happiness, Love & Wisdom* (Oakland: New Harbinger Publications, Inc., 2009),12.

13 Achor, *The Happiness Advantage*, 4.

14 Tolle, *The Power of Now*, 46.

15 Ibid, 63.

16 Roger Allen, "Life vs. Life Situation," *Roger K. Allen, PhD* (blog), https://www.rogerkallen.com/life-vs-life-situation/ .

17 Hanson and Mendius, *Buddha's Brain*, 41–42, 68.

18 Ibid, 51-52.

19 E. Maguire, D. Gadian, I. Johnsrude, C. Good, J. Ashburner, R. Frackowiak, and C. Frith, "Navigation-related structural change in the hippocampi of taxi drivers," *Proceedings of the National Academy of Sciences* 97 (2000): 4398–4403.

20 R. J. Davidson, "Well-being and affective style: Neural substrates and biobehavioural correlates," *Philosophical Transactions of the Royal Society* 359 (2004): 1395–1411, quoted in Hanson and Mendius, *Buddha's Brain*, 5.

21 Don Miguel Ruiz and Janet Mills, *The Four Agreements: A Toltec Wisdom Book* (San Rafael: Amber-Allen Publishing, Inc, 1997), 75–76.

22 Achor, *The Happiness Advantage*, front cover flap.

23 Maggie Fox, "Happiness is contagious: study," *Reuters*, December 4, 2008, https://www.reuters.com/article/us-happiness/happiness-is-contagious-study-idUSTRE4B400H20081205.

24 Achor, *The Happiness Advantage*, 109–110.

25 Stephen R. Covey, "Habit 2: Begin with the end in mind," *The 7 Habits of Highly Effective People: Powerful Lessons in Personal Change* (New York: Free Press, 1989).

26 Nanea Hoffman, "Notes from Nanea - The Deep End," *Sweatpants & Coffee*, accessed October 2020, https://www.sweatpantsandcoffee.com/note-from-nanea-the-deep-end/

27 Martin E. P. Seligman, T. A. Steen, N. Park, and C. Peterson, "Positive psychology progress: Empirical validation of interventions," *American Psychologist* (2005): 60, 410–421.

28 Robert A. Emmons and Robin Stern, "Gratitude as a Psychotherapeutic Intervention," *Journal of Clinical Psychology* 69 (June 17, 2013): 846–855, https://doi.org/10.1002/jclp.22020.

29 Shefali Tsabary, *The Conscious Parent: Transforming Ourselves, Empowering our Children* (Vancouver: Namaste Publishing, 2010).

30 "Albert Einstein > Quotes > Quotable Quote," Good Reads, Inc., https://www.goodreads.com/quotes/369-a-human-being-is-a-part-of-the-whole-called.

31 Sheryl Sandberg and Nell Scovell, *Lean In: Women, Work, and the Will to Lead* (New York: Alfred A. Knopf, 2013).

32 Christopher Bergland, "Having Social Bonds Is the No. 1 Way to Optimize Your Health," *Psychology Today*, January 14, 2016, https://www.psychologytoday.com/ca/blog/the-athletes-way/201601/having-social-bonds-is-the-no-1-way-optimize-your-health

33 Tsabary, *The Conscious Parent*, 209.

34 Master Mindset, "Natalie Davison - Living in Creativity – Master Mindset 2017." YouTube Video 28:32, March 6, 2018. https://www.youtube.com/watch?v=C2svX-IFxcg

35 TED, "The power of vulnerability | Brené Brown", YouTube Video 20:49, January 30, 2011. https://www.youtube.com/watch?v=iCvmsMzlF7o

36 William Strunk Jr. and E.B. White, *The Elements of Style* (Boston: Allyn & Bacon, 2000), 79.

37 Viktor E. Frankl, *Man's Search for Meaning* (Boston: Beacon Press, 1959), 67.

38 Eng, Kim. "Presence through Movement." Workshop, I am Genie, Toronto, June 3, 2018

39 Matt Atkinson, "Why is the UK So Unproductive Compared to Germany?" *Agency Central*, November 2016, https://www.agencycentral.co.uk/articles/2016-11/why-the-uk-is-much-less-productive-than-germany.htm

40 James M. Broadway, "Why Does Time Seem to Speed Up with Age?", *Scientific American*, July 1, 2016 https://www.scientificamerican.com/article/why-does-time-seem-to-speed-up-with-age/

41 Ibid.

42 Brené Brown, *Braving The Wilderness: The Quest for True Belonging and the Courage to Stand Alone*, (New York: Random House, 2017), 36-39

43 "Home > The Scout Promise and Law", Scouts, accessed October 2020 https://www.scout.org/promiseandlaw

44 Eckhart Tolle, *Stillness Speaks* (Vancouver: Namaste Publishing, 2003), 93.

45 "Calm-Meditate, Sleep, Relax", Calm.com Inc. Google Play App Store, version 5.4 (2020)

46 Andris Pone, *Attract: Power Up Your One-of-a-Kind Personal Brand* (Toronto: PPS Publishing, 2017), 32.

47 Oprah and Deepak, *21-Day Meditation Experience: Perfect Health*, https://chopracentermeditation.com/store/product/2

48 Quotefancy, https://quotefancy.com/quote/1596484/Robert-Morley-To-fall-in-love-with-yourself-is-the-first-secret-to-happiness, (accessed October 2020).

Biggleswade 5.89

Printed in Canada